Promotion Design 1

Promotion Design 1

The International Collection of Design for Promotion
Graphische Dokumente des täglichen Lebens
La Collection internationale du design promotionnel

Publisher and Creative Director: B. Martin Pedersen

Editors: Heinke Jenssen, April Heck
Assistant Editor: Chelsey Johnson

Art Director: Massimo Acanfora Graphic Designer: Dana Shimizu
Photographer: Alfredo Parraga

Published by Graphis Inc.

(Opposite) Design Firm, Client: Origin Design Company Ltd. Creative Director, Art Director: Robert Achten. Designer: Katherine Taylor. Photographer: Ian Robertson. *(following page)* Design Firm: Mires Design. Creative Director, Art Director, Designer: José A. Serrano. Illustrators: Tracy Sabin, Nancy Stahl. Client: Deleo Clay Tile Company. *(page 6)* Design Firm, Client: Meta-4, Inc.

Deleo Premium Quality Natural Clay Tiles
Deleo Premium Quality Natural Clay Tiles
Made From The Best Clay Available On Earth
DELEO
CLAY TILE COMPANY
Made In The USA
ICBO Approved

Contents Inhalt Sommaire

Remarks: We extend our heartfelt thanks to contributors throughout the world who have made it possible to publish a wide and international spectrum of the best work in the field of design. Entry instructions for all Graphis Books may be requested from: **Graphis Inc.**, 141 Lexington Avenue, New York, NY 10016-8193 or visit our Web site, www.graphis.com

Anmerkungen: Unser Dank gilt den Einsendern aus aller Welt, die es uns durch ihre Beiträge ermøglicht haben, ein breites, internationales Spektrum der besten Arbeiten zu veröffentlichen. Teilnahmebedingungen für die Graphis-Bücher sind erhältlich bei: **Graphis Inc.**, 141 Lexington Avenue, New York, NY 10016-8193. Besuchen Sie uns im World Wide Web, www.graphis.com

Remerciements: Nous remercions les participants du monde entier qui ont rendu possible la publication de cet ouvrage offrant un panorama complet des meilleurs travaux. Les modalités d'inscription peuvent être obtenues auprès de: **Graphis Inc.**, 141 Lexington Avenue, New York, NY 10016-8193. Rendez-nous visite sur notre site web: www.graphis.com

ISBN: 1-888001-61-5

Printed in Hong Kong by DNP.

We said
we'd give you a call.
One day soon,
we'll phone.
Meta-4

Commentary Kommentar Commentaire

During this holiday season,
let us consider how alike
one snowflake is to another,
rather than how different.
Cosgrove/Juro

Jerry Cosgrove: Seasonal Greetings

Each year since our agency was started in 1970, we've created and produced a mailing inspired by the spirit of the holiday season and our desire to offer greetings and best wishes to clients and colleagues. We mail a holiday ornament that's more than the conventional card, yet captures the tradition and warmth of the season. I like this tradition because it reminds us that graphic designers aren't—believe it or not—the center of the universe. It suggests that sources of good design can be found outside ourselves and our immediate, everyday surroundings and experience. It challenges us to look, and perhaps to leap, well beyond our creative conventions. I fondly recall, for instance, the year we mailed pine cones, each accompanied by the Legend of Pineas Cone—who finds "a proud and majestic evergreen that only Pineas could spruce up." We wanted to share the beauty of this simple, natural object with our friends, and make them smile. Another year we sent snowflakes, each one hand-crocheted by the mother of one of our designers.

Even years later, people told us how they remembered receiving their ornament and hanging it on their Christmas trees, how it was a reminder of simpler times.

We often find the spirit of the season in the icons of our childhood, like the year we sent toy drums, to help our recipients "be the hit of every Yuletide gathering." Or like the year we invited our friends to climb "aboard for the Holidays" on a miniature passenger train. Yet another year, we all scoured New York City for kids' mittens attached to woolen strings, to recall "the times when you trudged home, wet clear through your socks, your sled scraping the road where the plow scuffed off all the snow." We've sent red sleds ("for the hills you've yet to climb"), a battalion of toy nutcrackers (with "sugarplum visions of mouse tales"), and a stable of wooden rocking horses, each standing two inches high (to "gallop, stride, off into the sunset").

Sometimes the ornaments we find just seem to fit the occasion, like the tiny red mailbox complete with tiny holiday greetings, or the miniature antique globe ("Joy to the World"), or the festive brass horn to welcome the season with "plenty of hosting, toasting...and happy seasoning."

Admittedly, we're partial to outrageous puns—consider, for example, our fuzzy, miniature sheep with the message, "Humbug. Baaaah." Perhaps most outrageous was the greeting that accompanied last year's Santa Pez dispenser: "Pez on Earth." And yes, there may have been years we've gone over the top. We still talk about the year we mailed everyone on our list a "fish ruler," complete with instructions.

Occasionally, we've delivered a more reflective message, like the year we sent along a single sleigh bell, and invited our recipients to "Listen...and hear the season." Another year, (and another snowflake) we offered this lyrical suggestion: "During this holiday season, let us consider how alike one snowflake is to another, rather than how different."

We've discovered that everyone at the agency thoroughly enjoys working on our annual ornament program. In fact, it has become an agency-wide project. Each year, we put a selection of potential ornaments on display at the agency, and everyone votes for their favorite. Then we assign a designer and writer to transform the object, greeting, and packaging into a modest, compelling, and memorable gift.

Our creative teams consider this one of the most rewarding—and toughest—of assignments. There are no special formats or constraints; the message may be long or short, whimsical, even irreverent. In short, we want our package to be fresh and engaging; have an edge, yet be tasteful; stand out from the barrage of holiday mail; and, of course, make an enduring statement about the agency's creative excellence. This is, admittedly, quite a challenge!

Why take the time, trouble, and expense to create, produce, and mail almost a thousand packages each year? I like to think our holiday gifts stand in sharp contrast to the communication avalanche of phone calls, e-mails, voicemails, faxes, and machine-generated letters that inundate our colleagues throughout the year. I like to think that each package is a welcome special harbinger of the holidays. And I think it makes a strong, personal statement to our friends and associates about who we are as an agency, and, as importantly, who we are as people.

The folks who have received these ornaments continue to tell us that they save and cherish them for years. We think of that as our measure of success, and a good reason to keep the tradition going. Fortunately, we don't expect to run out of ideas for quite some time. Most of all, I think our holiday mailings are fun. They put all of us at the agency, and all of those who receive them, into good humor, the spirit of the season.

***Jerry Cosgrove** is president of Cosgrove Associates. Born and educated in Michigan, he has been a graphic designer and illustrator forever, working primarily in the financial, automotive, energy, and editorial fields. In 1970, he established Cosgrove Associates in New York City, focusing on marketing communications. He has been responsible for creating, developing, and implementing marketing programs for many leading product and service providers.*

PEZ ON EARTH

Rushing
Getting
Bringing
Wishing
Fanfaring
Dancing
Sharing
and...
A HORN
and plenty of

Rock—
—rock.
sunset.
CosgroveJuro

TOY
DRUM

(Opposite, top left)
"Pez on Earth. Dispensing holiday cheer and good wishes."

(Top right)
"A Horn, and Plenty of Hosting, Toasting, Feasting, Wrapping, Egg-Nogging..."

(Middle left)
"Joy to the World"

(Middle right)
"...He placed each treasured cone on a bough with a magician's touch...this one, here... that one, just over there."

(Bottom left)
"Rock-rock. Pony, ride. Giddy-up, get-along, gallop, stride...off into the sunset. JingleJangleJingle"

(Bottom right)
"Whether you're a musical prodigy or a fun-loving amateur, you'll be the hit of every Yuletide gathering."

(This page)
"Listen. Close your eyes and hear the season. Listen for the bells. Holiday bells. Church bells and jingle bells..."

Jerry Cosgrove: Weihnachts- und Neujahrsglückwünsche

Seit der Gründung unserer Agentur im Jahre 1970 haben wir uns jedes Jahr für die Weihnachtszeit etwas ausgedacht, um Kollegen und Kunden unsere guten Wünsche zu übermitteln. Wir verschicken etwas, das mehr als die übliche Karte ist, aber der Tradition und weihnachtlichen Stimmung entspricht. Mir gefällt diese Tradition, weil sie mich daran erinnert, dass wir Graphik-Designer – man mag es kaum für möglich halten – nicht der Nabel der Welt sind. Bei dieser Gelegenheit wird uns bewusst, dass gutes Design auch ausserhalb unseres Horizonts existiert; wir schauen uns um und gehen vielleicht sogar weit über unsere kreativen Gepflogenheiten hinaus. Ich denke gern an das Jahr, in dem wir Tannenzapfen verschickten, «den einzigartigen Schmuck des majestätischen, immergrünen Baumes».

Wir wollten unseren Freunden die Schönheit dieses schlichten Naturproduktes vor Augen führen und ihnen damit eine Freude machen. Ein anderes Mal verschickten wir Schneeflocken - jede einzelne von der Mutter eines unserer Designer gehäkelt.
Noch nach Jahren erzählen uns die Leute von dem Baumschmuck, den sie von uns bekommen haben. Sie haben ihn an ihren Weihnachtsbaum gehängt, und er hat sie an Zeiten erinnert, die einfacher zu sein schienen.
Oft sind es Dinge aus der Kindheit, die uns in Weihnachtsstimmung versetzen. Einmal wählten wir kleine Kindertrommeln, die die glücklichen Empfänger zum «Schlager eines jeden Weihnachtsfestes» machen sollten. Ein anderes Mal war es eine Spielzeugeisenbahn, und es hiess für unsere Freunde: «Ab in die Feiertage – alles einsteigen.». Und noch ein anderes Mal klapperten wir ganz New York ab, auf der Suche nach Kinderfäustlingen, die an einem Wollband festgemacht sind, um an die Zeiten zu erinnern, als man «von oben bis unten durchgenässt nach Hause zottelte, den Schlitten, der auf der schon freigeschaufelten Strasse schrappte, hinter sich herziehend. Wir verschickten rote Schlitten («für die Berge, die noch zu erklimmen sind»), ein Bataillon von Nussknackern (für «die süssesten Träume») und hölzerne Schaukelpferde, jedes 5cm hoch («um in die untergehende Sonne hinauszureiten»).
Manchmal finden wir auch Dinge, die für den Anlass genau richtig sind, wie der winzige rote Briefkasten mit noch winzigeren Weihnachtsgrüssen, oder die Miniaturausgabe einer alten Weltkugel ("Joy to the World"), oder das festliche Horn, das die Feiertage «mit viel Speis und Trank und lieben Gästen» ankündigt.
Zugegeben, uns machen freche Wortspiele Spass – zum Beispiel hatten wir einmal ein kleines, wolliges Schaf. Seine Botschaft war «Humbug. Määääh». Am frechsten war vielleicht der letzte Weihnachtsgruss, der den Santa Pez-Spender (Bonbonspender, oft in Form einer Comics-Figur) vom letzten Jahr begleitete: «Pez auf Erden!»
Es hat auch Jahre gegeben, in denen wir uns selbst übertroffen haben. Wir sprechen noch immer von dem Jahr, als jeder auf Instruktionen von uns bekam.
Manchmal hatten wir eine besinnlichere Botschaft; wir verschickten zum Beispiel ein Glöckchen, mit dem Versprechen: «Horcht ...und ihr werdet die Weihnachtszeit hören». In einem anderen Jahr nahmen wir wieder eine Schneeflocke: «Lasst uns während der Weihnachtstage daran denken, wie ähnlich eine Schneeflocke der anderen ist, nicht wie unähnlich.»
Wir haben festgestellt, dass es jedem in der Agentur Spass macht, an den Weihnachtsgrüssen zu arbeiten. Es beteiligen sich inzwi-schen alle. Jedes Jahr, wenn Weihnachten naht, schauen wir uns die verschiedenen Vorschläge in Form von Baumschmuck an, und dann wird abgestimmt. Danach werden ein Designer und ein Texter auserkoren, den Gegenstand, die Grussbotschaft und die Verpackung zu einem kleinen, unvergesslichen Geschenk zu machen.
Für unsere Kreativen ist das die dankbarste und schwierigste aller Aufgaben. Es gibt keine vorgegebenen Formate oder Einschränkungen; die Botschaft kann lang oder kurz sein, ein bisschen verrückt oder sogar respektlos. Alles, was wir möchten, ist eine frische, packende Sache mit einem Clou, die geschmackvoll ist, und sich von den vielen anderen Weihnachtsgrüssen abhebt; dabei soll sie natürlich auch Ausdruck der Kreativität unserer Agentur sein. Keine leichte Aufgabe also!
Warum nimmt man sich die Zeit und scheut weder Mühe noch Kosten für Herstellung und Versand von jährlich fast tausend Päckchen? Ich hoffe, dass unsere kleinen Weihnachtsgeschenke sich von den Anrufen, E-mails, Voicemails, Faxen und Computerbriefen, die das ganze Jahr über auf unsere Kollegen niederprasseln, wohltuend unterscheiden. Ich hoffe, dass jedes einzelne Päckchen als spezieller Vorbote der Weihnachtszeit willkommen ist. Und ich glaube, dass wir damit unseren Freunden und Partnern auf spezielle Weise sagen, wer wir sind – als Agentur und als Menschen. Alle, die unseren Baumschmuck bekommen haben, erzählen uns, dass sie ihn jahrelang sorgsam aufheben. Das ist für uns der Massstab des Erfolgs und ein guter Grund, die Tradition beizubehalten. Wir nehmen nicht an, dass uns die Ideen so bald ausgehen werden.
Ich glaube, dass unsere Weihnachtsgrüsse vor allem Spass machen. Sie sorgen für Weihnachtsstimmung, nicht nur bei den Empfängern, auch bei uns in der Agentur!

***Jerry Cosgrove** hat lange als Graphiker und Illustrator gearbeitet - seine Kunden waren in erster Linie Redaktionen und Unternehmen aus dem Finanzbereich sowie der Auto- und Treibstoffbranche. 1970 gründete er Cosgrove Associates in New York, die sich auf Marketing-Kommunikation spezialisiert haben. Jerry Cosgrove hat inzwischen für zahlreiche fuhrende Hersteller und Service-Unternehmen Marketing- und Verkaufsprogramme entwickelt und ausgeführt.*

Jerry Cosgrove: vœux de fin d'année

Depuis la fondation de notre agence en 1970, nous essayons chaque année de trouver une idée originale pour souhaiter nos vœux de fin d'année à nos clients et collègues. Nous n'envoyons pas une simple carte de vœux, mais une décoration qui s'inscrit dans la tradition de Noël et en reflète l'atmosphère. J'apprécie cette tradition car, que vous le croyez ou non, elle nous rappelle à nous autres, designers graphiques, que nous ne sommes pas le nombril du monde. A cette occasion, nous prenons conscience que le design graphique s'étend à d'autres domaines qu'à notre environnement quotidien et immédiat. Nous regardons alors au-delà de notre horizon et allons parfois jusqu'à transgresser les règles en vigueur dans notre travail créatif.

Je repense avec joie à cette année où nous avions envoyé des pommes de pin, ces «ornements uniques qui parent l'épicéa majestueux, éternellement vert». Nous voulions rendre nos amis attentifs à la beauté de ce simple fruit de la nature et, bien entendu, leur faire plaisir. Une autre année, notre choix s'est arrêté sur des flocons de neige, tous tricotés avec le plus grand soin par la mère de l'un de nos designers.

Bien des années plus tard, les gens nous parlent encore de cette décoration qu'ils ont utilisée pour leur sapin de Noël, une décoration d'une époque révolue où tout paraissait plus simple.

Souvent, ce sont les objets de notre enfance qui rappellent à notre mémoire l'atmosphère de Noël. Une année, ce furent des tambours pour enfants qui devaient aider l'heureux destinataire à «faire la fête tambour battant». Une autre, des petits trains avec le message «En voiture! Cap sur les vacances!». Une autre encore, nous avons parcouru tout New York à la recherche de moufles pour enfants attachés ensemble par un cordon de laine, un «souvenir des jours heureux où l'on traînait les pieds en rentrant à la maison, mouillés de la tête aux pieds, tirant derrière soi une vieille luge qui raclait la chaussée fraîchement déblayée». Nous avons envoyé des luges rouges pour «les sommets qui restent à gravir», un bataillon de casse-noisettes avec des «visions de friandises et de douceurs pour devenir tout sucre tout miel» et des chevaux à bascule en bois d'une hauteur de 5 cm pour «partir au galop dans les lueurs du soleil couchant».

Il nous arrive de temps à autre de dénicher des objets qui s'inscrivent parfaitement dans la tradition, comme ces petites boîtes aux lettres rouges arborant des vœux de Noël encore plus minuscules, ou cette version miniature d'un globe ancien «Joy to the World», ou encore cette corne d'abondance annonçant les heureuses prémices de «ces fêtes où l'on peut ensemble boire et manger jusqu'à satiété».

Nous avons aussi un penchant pour la plaisanterie, comme lorsque nous avons envoyé un mouton à la toison abondante, pâle imitation du Père Noël, avec le message «Charlatanisme! Beeeeeeh!». La plus loufoque était sans doute celle de l'année dernière, qui accompagnait le Santa Pez (minidistributeur de bonbons à l'image d'un personnage de dessins animés): «Pez sur Terre».

Notre imagination débridée nous amène parfois à dépasser un peu les bornes. Nous parlons volontiers de l'année où nous avons envoyé à tous ceux qui figuraient sur notre liste une règle en forme de poisson avec son mode d'emploi. Certaines années, nos créations reflètent mieux cette période propice au recueillement, comme cette clochette assortie de l'invitation «Ouvrez tout grand vos oreilles et écoutez la magie de Noël!». Une autre fois, nous avons repris l'idée du flocon de neige: «Durant ces fêtes de fin d'année, n'oublions pas de penser à quel point chaque flocon de neige se ressemble et oublions les différences.»

Nous avons constaté que tous les collaborateurs de l'agence prennent énormément de plaisir à chercher une formule originale pour adresser nos vœux de fin d'année. C'est devenu un projet auquel chacun participe de son mieux. A l'approche des fêtes, nous passons en revue les différentes décorations proposées et en élisons une après un vote démocratique. Ensuite, nous choisissons un designer et un rédacteur publicitaire dont la tâche consiste à trouver un message et à créer un emballage afin que cette petite attention se transforme en un cadeau inoubliable. Pour nos créatifs, ce travail est à la fois des plus agréables et des plus difficiles. Aucun format ni aucune restriction ne sont imposés. Le message peut être court ou long, un peu fou ou irrespectueux. Ce que nous voulons, c'est une attention qui marque le coche, quelque chose de frais et d'élégant, quelque chose qui reflète notre créativité.

Mais pourquoi consacrer autant de temps et d'argent à la préparation et à l'envoi de quelque mille paquets par an? J'espère que, contrairement à tous ces e-mails, fax et lettres qui s'abattent sur nos collègues tout au long de l'année, nos petits cadeaux de Noël leur apportent un moment de bonheur. Et je crois que de cette façon, nous disons à nos amis et clients qui nous sommes en tant qu'agence et en tant qu'êtres humains. Tous les destinataires de ces petites attentions nous racontent qu'ils les conservent précieusement. C'est à cela que nous mesurons notre succès, et c'est aussi une excellente raison de perpétuer cette tradition. Et nous ne sommes pas près d'être à court d'idées. Je crois que nos vœux de fin d'année procurent avant tout plaisir. Ils contribuent à la magie de Noël, pas seulement auprès de nos clients, mais aussi au sein de l'agence.

***Jerry Cosgrove**, le directeur de Cosgrove Associates, a toujours travaillè comme desi-gner graphique et illustrateur. Dans un premier temps, il exerçait ses activités dans les domaines rédactionnel, automobile et énergétique. En 1970, il a fondé l'agence Cosgrove Associates à New York spécialisée dans la communication marketing. Il s'est chargè de la crèation, du développement et de la mise en place de programmes marketing et de vente pour différents produits et prestataires de services.*

(Previous spread, left page)
Portrait of Jerry Cosgrove, courtesy of Cosgrove Associates, Inc.

(Opposite)
"A shiny red sled for the hills you've yet to climb... with warmest holiday wishes."

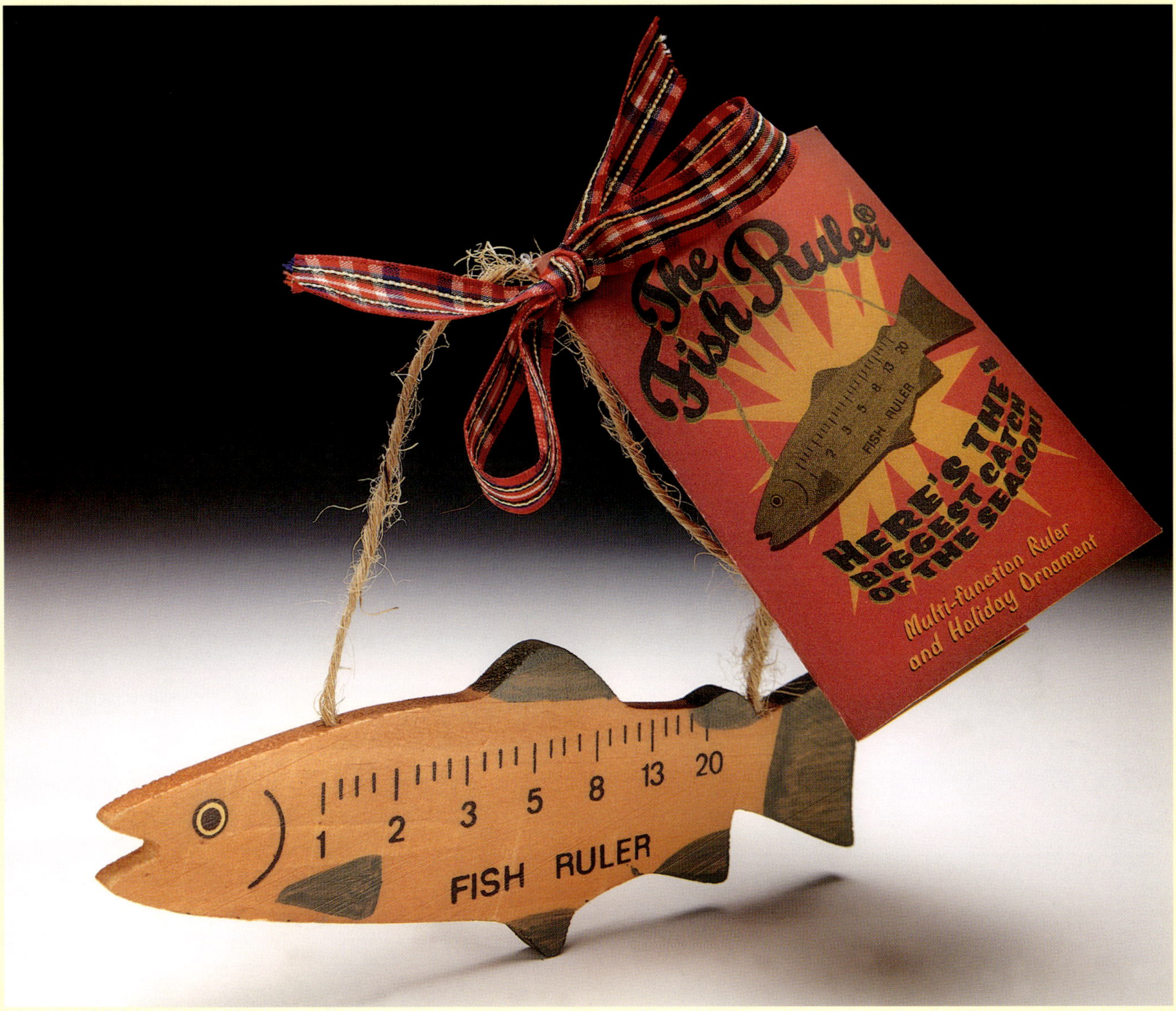

(This page)
"...Please note, if you already have a measuring device, throw it away and replace it with this all-natural wood product which also acts as a unique holiday ornament."

(Following page)
"Happy Holidays and a first class New Year."

Promotion Design 1

Cesar Pelli Buildings & Thoughts Wednesday October 25, 1995 6:00 pm Cooper-Hewitt, National Design Museum

DEADLINE

for contributions to the second issue of AGITATE, the newsletter of the AGI, is October 31st. Please send them to David Hillman Pentagram Design, 11 Needham Road, London W11 2RP, England

TITANIC

A WHITE STAR LINER
NEW YORK, N.Y.

March 15, 1912

Dear Sir:

Thank you for your interest in traveling aboard the Titanic. Unfortunately, our maiden voyage (April 14, 1912), has been sold out. Please try us again at a later date.

Mary Woolrich

Mary Woolrich
Reservations Dept.

(Opposite)
Design Firm, Client: Bailey Lauerman & Associates
Creative Director: Rich Bailey
Art Director: Sean Faden
Writers: Mitch Koch, Doug Cook
Photographer: Roger Barnes
Description: One of a series of imaginative cards from a boxed set sent to clients at Christmastime.

(This page)
Design Firm, Client: Nike, Inc.
Art Director: Jeff Weithman
Designer: Clint Gorthy

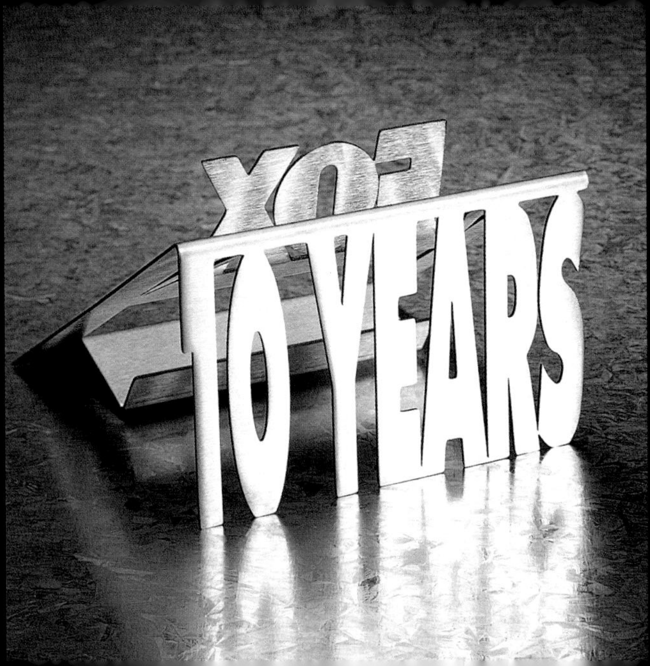
10 YEARS

FOX
THE LEGENDS AWARD
For extraordinary contributions to the growth of the FOX Network
Presented January 11, 1997 to:
Michael Finkelstein
Chairman and CEO
Renaissance Communications Corporation

Design Firm:
Antista Fairclough Design
Creative Directors, Art Directors,
Designers: Tom Antista,
Thomas Fairclough
Photography:
Michael West Photography
Client: Creative Club of Atlanta

Design Firm: Sayles Graphic Design
Creative Director, Art Director,
Designer: John Sayles
Writer: Annie Meacham

Metal Fabricator:
Iowa Metal Fabrication
Client: American Cancer Society

Design Firm: Hornall Anderson
Design Works
Art Director: Jack Anderson
Designers: Jack Anderson, Cliff Chung
Client: Microsoft

Design Firm: Design Guys
Creative Director, Art Director,
Designer: Steven Sikora
Client: Take 5 on First

FACE.
hairstyling by
antti haakana
(90) 626 358
pohjois-esplanadi 33 a 2. krs

(Opposite)
Garage Graphics
Creative Director, Art Director,
Designer: Rikard Lassenius
Client: Face

(This page)
Garage Graphics
Creative Director, Art Director,
Designer: Rikard Lassenius
Photographer: Ryushi Nakagawa
Client: Nail Design

Will she be the first woman to walk on Mars?

?

(This spread)
Design Firm: Sullivan Perkins
Art Directors: Ron Sullivan,
Dan Richards
Designer, Illustrator: Dan Richards

Will she win a gold medal at the Olympics in 2012?

Will she appear in the Grand Opera as a *prima donna*?

Will she grow up to be President?
INS THE

Will she ever sleep through the night?
Rachel Elizabeth Brown was born January 29, 1994 at 12:45 P.M.
She's the answer to all of Amy and David's wishes for a beautiful and healthy baby girl.

(This page)
Design Firm: Willoughby Design
Creative Director, Art Director,
Designer: Garrett Burke
Photographer: Mike Bryan

Thank you!
Family Lynch-Imhasly, Blattenstrasse 72, 3904 Naters, Switzerland.
The day Jana Fiona was born . . .
. . . Frank saw everything through rose-coloured glasses . . .
. . . Astrid was pink with pride . . .
. . . and Elena was a little green with envy.
In fact, just about everything has been a little more colourful!
Thank you!
Family Lynch-Imhasly, Blattenstrasse 72, 3904 Naters, Switzerland.

What's sweet, weighs 5 pounds, and was delivered on Valentine's Day?

Sophie Joseph Schwartz

February 14, 1995

5 pounds, 1/2 ounce

(This spread)
Creative Director,
Designer: Scott Paramski
Art Directors: Sean Patrick,
Scott Paramski
Writer: Sean Patrick

Photographer: Robert Millman
Client: Heitman Financial/
Snowmass Land Co.
Description: Gift to purchasers
of real estate.

(Following spread, left page)
Design Firm: Art Force Studio
Creative Director: Attila Simon
Art Director, Designer,
Illustrator: Tamás Veress
Description: Greeting cards
for clients for "name day."

ÜDVÖZLŐ
ART FORCE No1
DESIGN
KÖSZÖNTI
AZ ART FORCE
SZEMÉLYZETE
KÉRJÜK FOGADJA EL TŐLÜNK
EZT A CSEKÉLYSÉGET
HÖLGYEM
URAM
A SZEMÉLYZET

LA LLAMA
CONTENIDO NETO: 40 FOSFOROS
R.D. 063755
PERU

(Previous page, this and following spread)
Design Firm: Paper House Productions
Designer: Jeffrey Milstein
Photographers: Dan Lavoie, Al Seib,
Jeffrey Milstein

FOLDING CARD
HAPPY
BIRTHDAY

Boretti Designs, Ltd.
Art Director, Designer, Product
Photographer: Roberto Klachky
Client: México En Papel
Description: Card/photo frame

(This spread)
Design Firm: Gill Fishman Associates
Art Director, Designer: Gill Fishman
Illustrator, Photographer:
Alicia Ozyjowski
Client: Museum School

Inspired Ideas • Tangible Gifts • Labors of Love

Cocktails and Conversation
Snapshots and Photos
Food and Frolic

(This spread)
Design Firm: Carbone Smolan Associates
Creative Director: Leslie Smolan
Art Director: Jennifer Domer
Designer: Lesley Feldman
Photographer: Peter Medilek
Client: San Francisco International Airport
Description: Books of postcards for exhibitions hosted by the San Francisco Airports Commission

Tricky Taxis, early 1950s, Marx, United States, lithographed tin. Collection of Nathan Willensky, New York.

During the twentieth century tin toys came to dominate the world of toymaking. Made of two or more pieces stamped out by machine, they are assembled by hand using a solder or bent-tab method. They were painted by hand until the invention of offset lithography. Marx is noted for its wind-up toys. The *Tricky Taxi* was produced just prior to Marx's switch to plastic from tin. Wound with a key, it will go to the edge of a table, stop, and not fall off.

TO

October 1994 — February 1995, San Francisco International Airport.

The San Francisco Airports Commission presents: Hailing Taxis

fication models. He recalls that he would frequently look at those models and think about the important part they had played in America's war effort. This led to his eventual decision to put together a major collection of World War II aircraft recognition artifacts. Today it is the largest known collection of its kind in the world. It includes over twelve hundred spotter models and thousands of manuals, posters, and other wartime aircraft identification training aids.

Mr. Winston states: In the first order of things, models and toys have connotation of play. In fact, this collection began as boyhood toys. Although they fantasize about it, most American children mercifully do not know war. Only years later did I come to understand the use of these objects: the primitive distinction of friend from foe. In this sense they become beautiful — not truly toys, not obvious war implements. And now, some fifty years after World War II, they regain some of their innocence, representing as they do, a sad time passed, as a memory of war, but also a symbol of peace. And thus, these objects regain their innocence as boyhood remembrances.

Ronald Winston is President and Chairman of the Board of Harry Winston, Inc. A graduate of Harvard, Mr. Winston is also a scientist whose work in the field of aerospace propulsion has earned him numerous honors, including the esteemed American Rocket Society Award. Tom Stern is the curator of Mr. Winston's collection. Mr. Stern is a writer and former cable television marketing executive.

mental simulation, and interactive audio and video components.

Paul Neuman's involvement with worlds in miniature began in childhood with the construction of an extensive miniature railroad. He bought his first set of architectural building blocks nine years ago and became an avid collector after seeing the collection of Norman Brosterman.

Mr. Neuman feels that the pieces in his collection often straddle the line between folk art and toys. He considers F. Ad. Richter to be the creator of the ultimate in building toys, the complexity, detail, texture, and color being far beyond that of any other manufacturer.

Mr. Neuman is particularly involved in the details of the construction. He enjoys the challenge presented by sets that do not necessarily correspond to the box illustration and by sets that have no accompanying instruction sheets.

For him one of the most fascinating aspects of collecting is the continuous discovery of new examples offering a chance to discover new buildings and new worlds in miniature.

Paul Neuman studied architecture and civil engineering and has an MFA in glass and sculpture. He continues to make sculpture, is a caterer and runs a retail specialty food store, and considers himself to be a frustrated toy designer and manufacturer. He has designed building block toys, many of which are variations on ones in his collection.

(This spread)
Design Firm: IMA-Press Publishers
Art Directors, Designers:
Andre Shelutto, Igor Gurovich
Client: IMA Press Association
Description: Postcards

ДАН
ПРИКАЗ
ЕМУ
НА ЗАПАД
ЕЙ
В ДРУГУЮ СТОРОНУ

ПОМНИШЬ
ТОВАРИЩ
КАК ВМЕСТЕ
СРАЖАЛИСЬ
КАК НАС
ОБНИМАЛА
ГРОЗА

D I O R A M A
A
FOLD
ALASKA BROWN BEAR
American Museum of Natural History
D
A
FOLD
CHEETAH
American Museum of Natural History
A M A
A
FOLD
OSBORN CARIBOU
American Museum of Natural History

(This spread)
Design Firm: Paper House Productions
Creative Director, Art Director,
Designer, Illustrator: Jeffrey Milstein
Client: American Museum of
Natural History
Description: Cards turn into dioramas
with a simple fold.

(This page)
Design Firm: Energy Project
Art Director: Nikko Amandonico
Designer: Rachel Wild
Client: Benetton Group

(Opposite)
Design Firm, Client: Mires Design Inc.
Creative Director,
Art Director: John Ball
Designer: Deborah Hom
Illustrator: Tracy Sabin
Writer: Brian Woolsey
Printer: Hal Truschke

Thanks a ton.

In appreciation of all those who've helped us to have a happy and prosperous 1996, we at Mires Design have donated more than a ton of turkeys to feed the homeless this holiday season.

(This spread)
Design Firm, Client: The Sloan Group
Creative Directors: Cliff Sloan,
Wyndy Wilder
Designer: Shawn Markert

Send some holiday cheer
with these swell cards!
Compliments of:
the SLOAN Group
Creativity for contemporary marketers.
A Merry Christmas
Seasons Greetings
A happy New Year
A Jolly Time
To You This New Year

Every year at this time designers all over the world are struggling with the dilemma of what to do about their Holiday Greetings. Should it be an object or a card? Should it be gimmicky or traditional? An intricate die-cut or maybe a bottle of wine with a fancy custom label? Should it be engraved or embossed? How much should we spend? Should we even do a card? Maybe just tell everyone we were just too busy with work and all. What will our clients think? What will our friends and colleagues say? Will it win any design awards? While what we really want to do is to wish everyone a Joyous Holiday Season and a Healthy and Happy New Year. So, from all of us at Eric Baker Design Associates, we hope your Holidays are filled with Happiness, Peace and Good Health.

Design Firm, Client:
Evenson Design Group
Creative Director: Stan Evenson
Designer: Amy Hershman
Photographer: Anthony Nex
Printer: Anderson Printing

☐ Fröhliche Weihnachten ☐ Merry Christmas ☐ Een vrolijk kerstfeest ☐ Felices Navidades ☐ Joyeux Noël ☐ Feliz Natal ☐ Felice Natale

ZANDERS

Printed on CHROMOLUX 700, 250 g/m^2

C M Y K

☐ Gutes neues Jahr ☐ Happy New Year ☐ Gelukkig nieuwjaar ☐ Próspero año nuevo ☐ Bonne année ☐ Bom Ano Novo ☐ Buon anno

ZANDERS

C
M
Y
K

Design Firm, Client:
Sietsema Engel & Partners
Designer: In-house

Design Firm: Tangram
Strategic Design
Creative Director, Writer:
Enrico Sempi
Art Directors: Enrico Sempi,
Antonella Trevisan
Designer: Antonella Trevisan
Description: Gift of incense

(This spread)
Design Firm: Richards Group
Creative Director: Stan Richards
Art Director: Jason Stanfield
Writer: Chad Swisher
Contributors: Kelly Andrews, Jeff Hopfer, Mark McKenzie, Jed Schroeder, Kevin Swisher

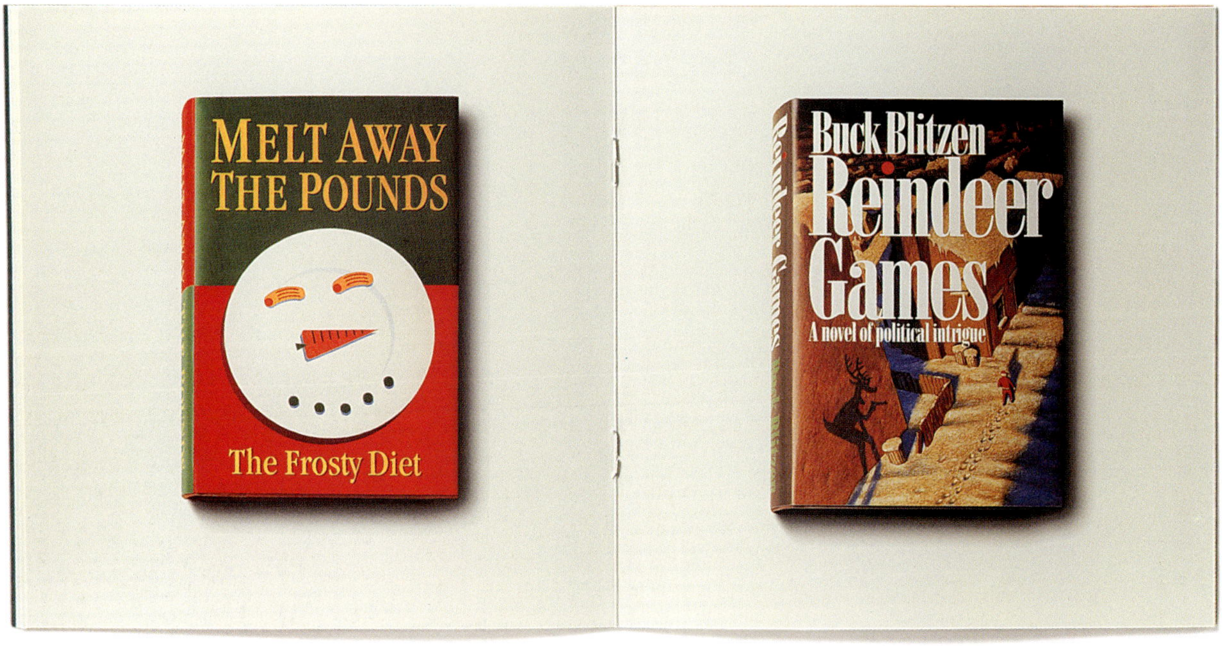

WHO-VILLE'S #1 BEST-SELLER
THE HO HO HEIST
HOW I PULLED OFF THE CRIME OF THE CENTURY
BY THE GRINCH
Same Time Next Year
A TALE OF PASSION, LONGING AND MISTLETOE

THROUGH THE FOG
A SHINING EXAMPLE OF OVERCOMING A HANDICAP
AN AUTOBIOGRAPHY BY RUDOLPH
THE REAL RUDOLPH
PORTRAIT OF A RED-NOSER
BY PRANCER

REMEMBER, NO MATTER HOW CRASS AND COMMERCIALIZED THE HOLIDAYS HAVE BECOME, IT COULD BE WORSE.
SEASON'S GREETINGS FROM ALL OF US AT
THE RICHARDS GROUP

(This page)
Design Firm, Client: Studio Bubblan
Art Director: Jeannette Palmqvist
Designer: Kari Palmqvist

(Opposite)
Design Firm, Client: Designframe
Creative Director, Art Director,
Designer: Michael McGinn

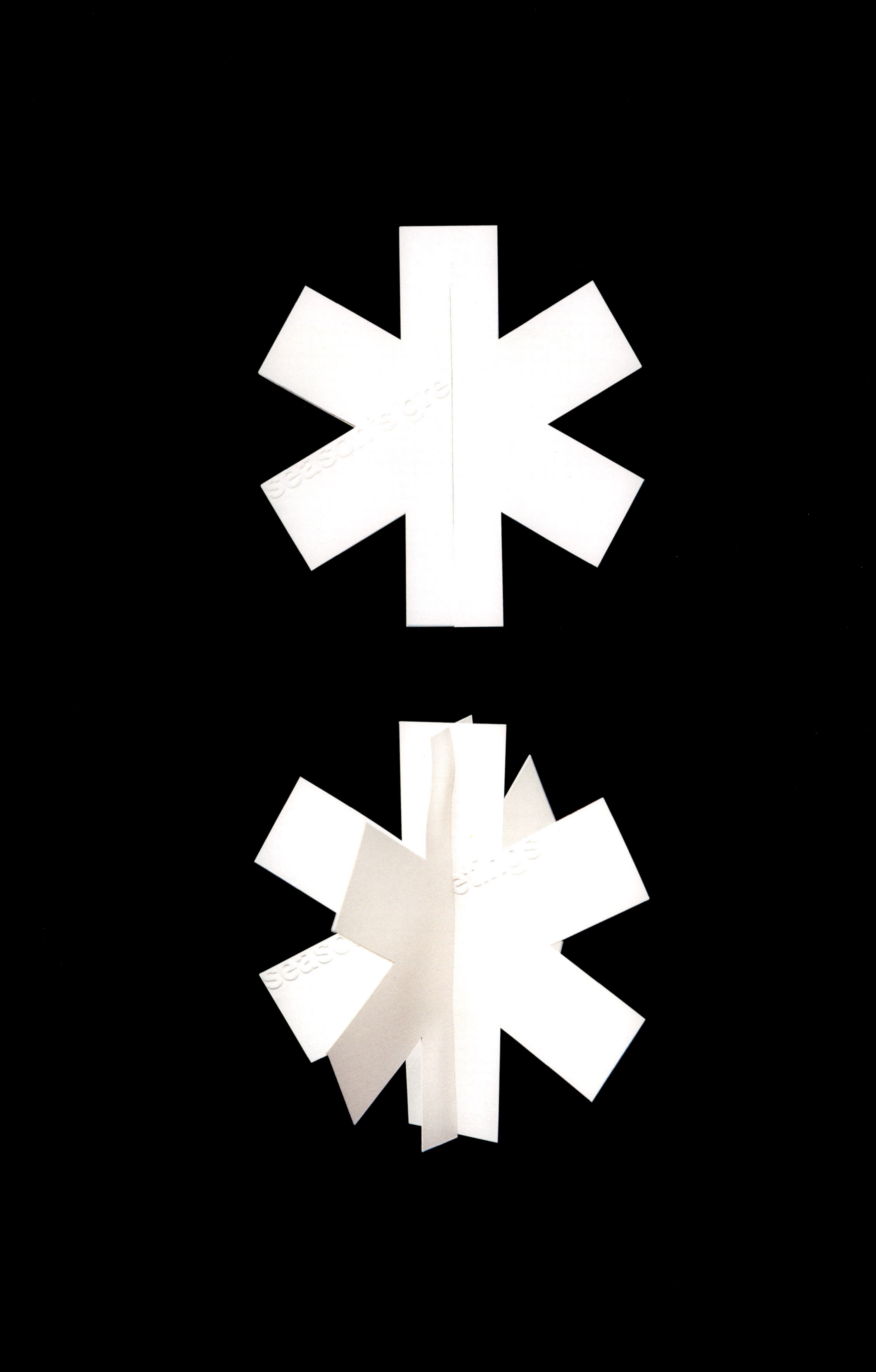

This holiday season
we would like to share
a little...

love...

and peace...

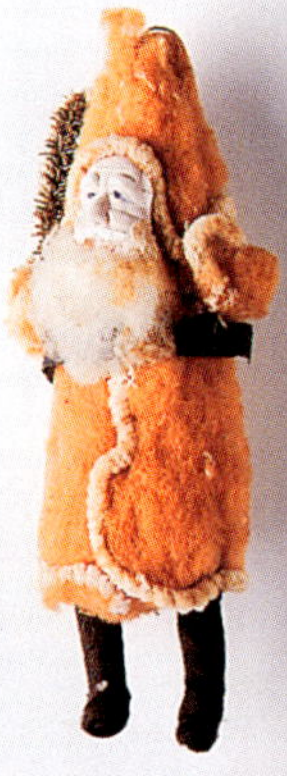

ROGER

Cook and Shanosky Associates, Inc.

(Opposite)
Design Firm, Client: Cook and Shanosky Associates
Creative Director, Art Director, Photographer: Roger Cook
Designers: Roger Cook, Michael Milligan
Writer: Michael Milligan

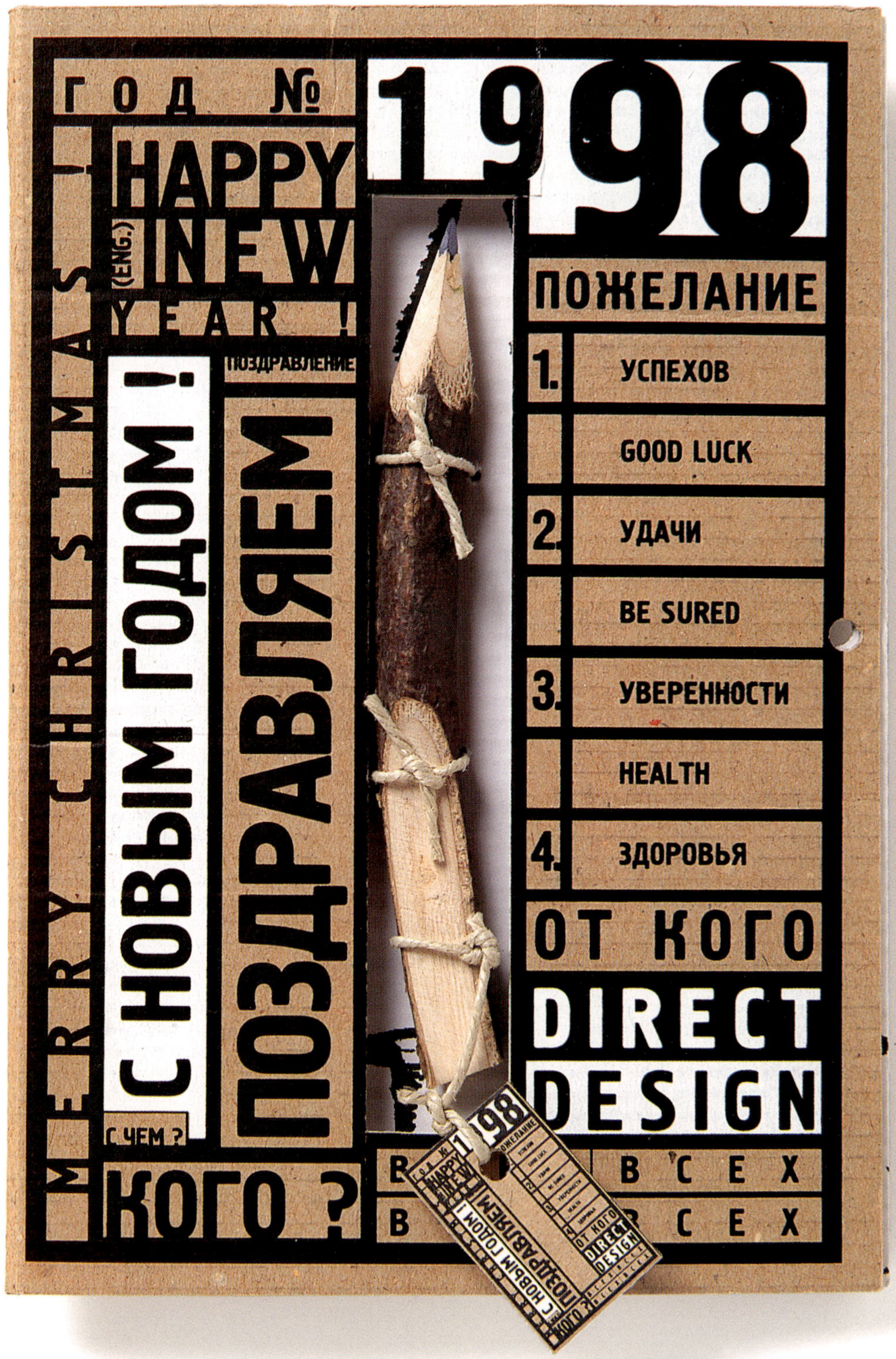

(This page)
Design Firm, Client: Direct Design
Designers: Dmitry Pioryshkov, Leon Feigin

ICL
by Sazaby
SAZABY Inc.
4-18-11, Minami-Aoyama,
Minato-ku, Tokyo, 107
Telephone 03-5412-1834
merry christmas
ICL
SEASON'S GREETINGS

NO.EL
NO.EL
NO.EL
NO.EL

Pressley Jacobs Design
Stamp Collection
PRESSLEY JACOBS DESIGN INC.
1985-1995
10 YEARS

make a JOYful noise
bring JOY to the world
enJOY the season
the JOY of sharing

(This page)
Design Firm, Client: Sazaby Inc.
Designer: In-house

(Opposite)
Design Firm, Client:
M Skjei Design Co.
Art Director, Designer:
Michael Skjei
Printer: Pentagram Press

1936
HOLIDAY GREETINGS
1939
The first Christmas Seals were created in 1904 by a Danish postal clerk named Einar Holboell.
His Seals sold for a penny each, raising $18,000 to help tubercular children. In 1996 over 80 countries sponsored Christmas Seals raising many millions
($27 million in the U.S. alone) to help combat respiratory diseases. Amazing how licking something so small can help
M. Skjei Design Co.

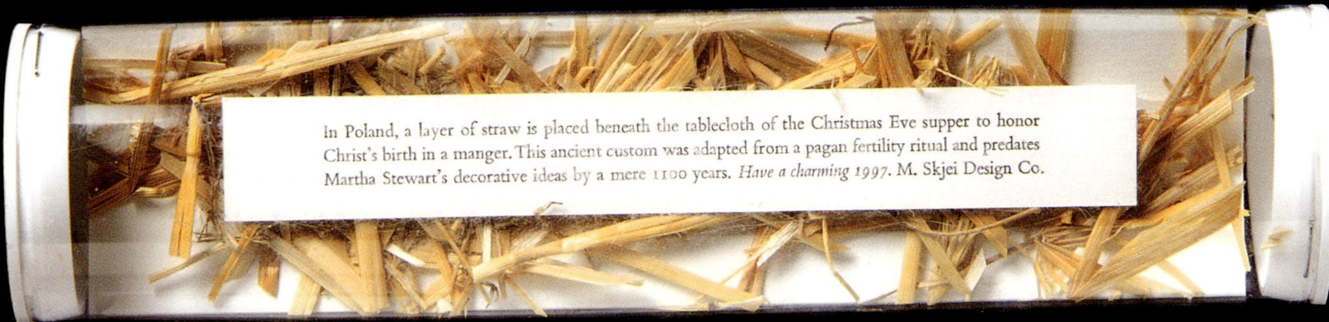
In Poland, a layer of straw is placed beneath the tablecloth of the Christmas Eve supper to honor
Christ's birth in a manger. This ancient custom was adapted from a pagan fertility ritual and predates
Martha Stewart's decorative ideas by a mere 1100 years. *Have a charming 1997.* M. Skjei Design Co.

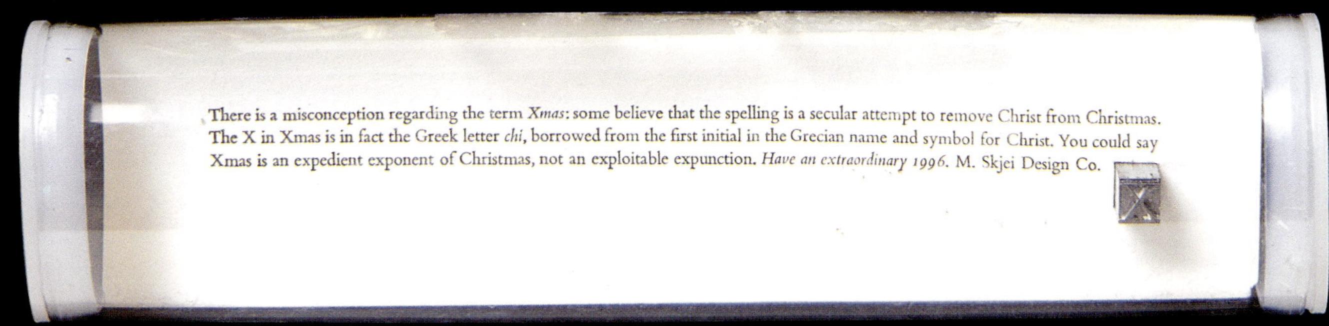
There is a misconception regarding the term *Xmas*: some believe that the spelling is a secular attempt to remove Christ from Christmas.
The X in Xmas is in fact the Greek letter *chi*, borrowed from the first initial in the Grecian name and symbol for Christ. You could say
Xmas is an expedient exponent of Christmas, not an exploitable expunction. *Have an extraordinary 1996.* M. Skjei Design Co.

A merrie Christmas.

maria cristina romagnoli grafica

via massaciuccoli 12 00199 roma tel 06/ 86.21.82.60

SNIFF, SNIFF
SNORT, SNORT
GRUNT, GRUNT
OINK, OINK!
GUNG HAY FAT CHOY
HAPPY CHINESE NEW YEAR 4693 A.D.
YEAR OF THE PIG
WISHING YOU GOOD HEALTH AND PROSPERITY
RUSSELL LEONG DESIGN

(Opposite)
Design Firm, Client:
Russell Leong Design
Art Director, Designer, Illustrator:
Russell Leong
Printer: QSP Printing
Description: Chinese Lunar
New Year's Card

(This page)
Design Firm: Art Force Studio
Creative Director: Attila Simon
Art Directors, Designers:

(This page)
Design Firm, Client: Cosgrove Juro
Description: 1998
Holiday Greeting to clients

(Opposite)
Design Firm, Client:
Cento Per Cento Design
Designer: Pier Paolo Pitacco

PACE e BENE
1996!
Pier Paolo Pitacco

Design Firm: RBMM/
The Richards Group
Art Director, Designer: Dick Mitchell
Illustrator: Wayne Johnson
Client: RBMM

Design Firm, Client: Peterson & Co.
Art Director, Designer, Illustrator,
Writer: Scott Ray

Design Firm, Client:
Seman Design Group
Art Director, Designer:
Richard M. Seman
Photographer: Walt Seng
Writer: Ron Seman

Design Firm, Client:
Henderson/Cartledge Photography
Creative Directors, Art Directors,
Designers, Writers:
Elizabeth Henderson, David Cartledge
Photography: Henderson/
Cartledge Photography

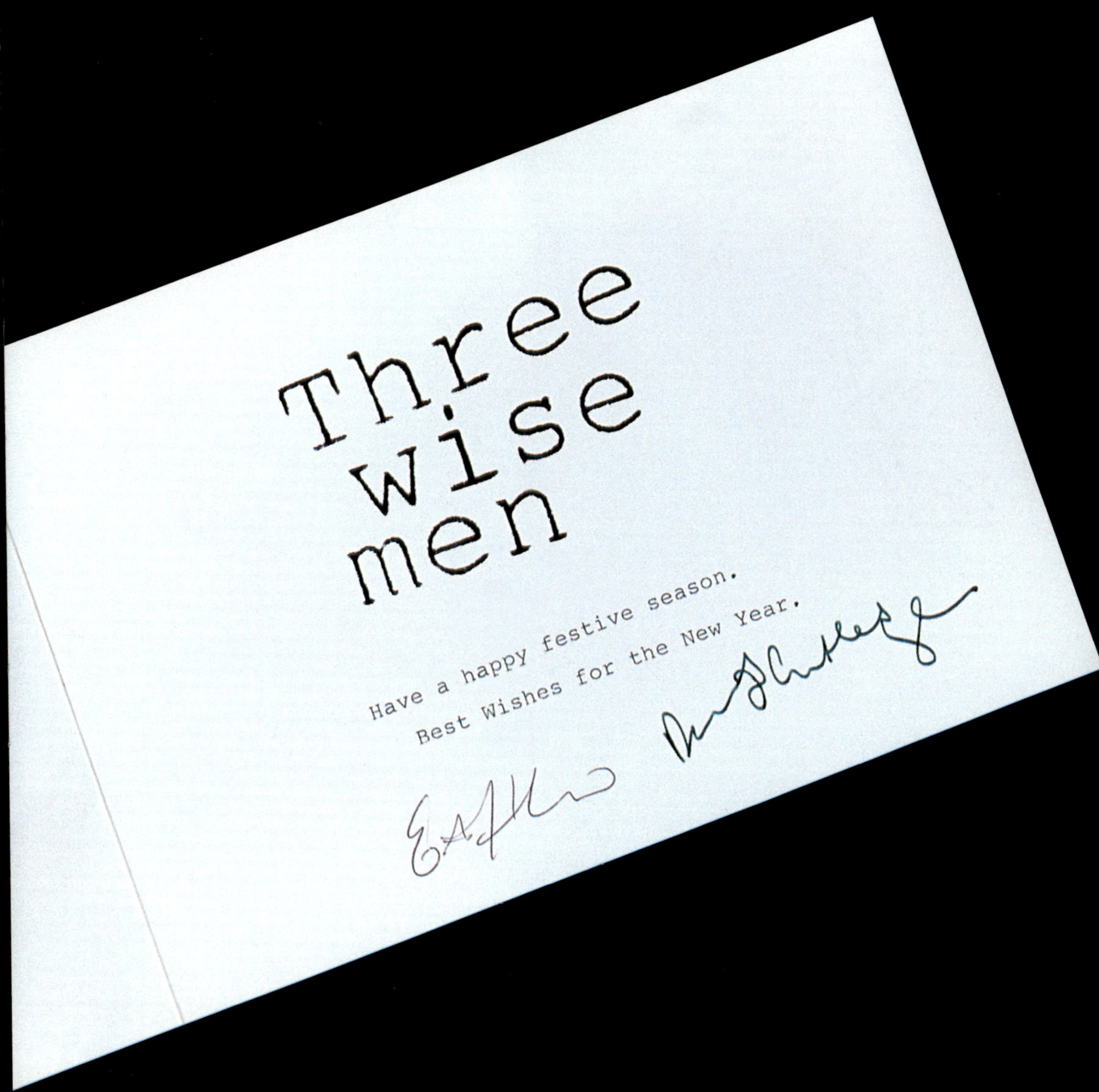

(This spread)
Design Firm, Client:
GibbsBaronet
Creative Director,
Art Director:
Willie Baronet

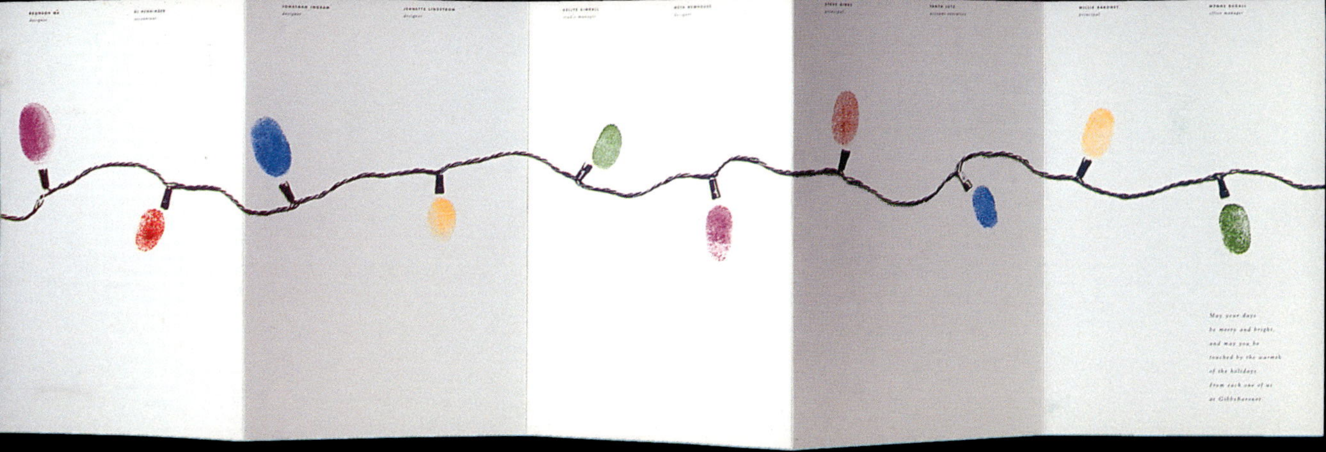
May your days
be merry and bright,
and may you be
touched by the warmth
of the holidays
from each one of us
at GibbsBaronet

SEASONS GREETINGS

FROM EVERYONE AT
THE CONTAINER STORE

(Opposite)
Design Firm: Sibley/Peteet Design
Art Director, Designer, Writer,
Illustrator: Rex Peteet
Client: The Container Store

(This page)
Designer, Illustrator,
Client: Peter Krämer

(This spread)
Design Firm, Client:
North American Packaging Corp.
Creative Director, Art Director,
Designer: John DeStefano
Description: Emergency Shopping Bag

Design Firm: Nike Image Design
Art Director: Valerie Taylor Smith
Designer: Michael Hernandez
Illustrator: Terry Allen
Writer: Bob Lambie
Client: Nike, Inc.

Design Firm: Via Design Inc.
Art Director: Lee Perrault
Illustrator: David M. Carroll
Photographer: Brian Wilder
Writers: Lee Perrault,
Richard W. Moore
Client: Audubon Society of
New Hampshire

(This page)
Design Firm: Ritta & Associates
Creative Director: Michael Tobin
Designers: Sheila Smith, MaryEllen Vander Brink
Photographers: Bill Cash, Guy Spangenberg
Writers: Catherine Armstrong, Vicki List
Client: BMW of North America

(Opposite)
Design Firm: Duffy Design Firm
Art Director: Dan Olson
Designers: Dan Olson, Todd Bartz, Eden Fahlen
Photographer: Lev Tushavs
Client: Flagstone Brewery

FIRST RESERVE
LAGER
BOTTLED
IN U.S.A.
A beer as bold as the events that inspired it.
FLAGSTONE BREWERY
SALEM, N.C.
FLAGSTONE BREWERY
Drawer T, Salem Station
Winston-Salem, N.C. 27108
54-22
FIRST RESERVE
LAGER
BOTTLED
IN U.S.A.
FLAGSTONE BREWERY
FIRST RESERVE
LAGER
BOTTLED
IN U.S.A.

DELEO CLAY TILE
SINCE 1984
QUALITY CRAFTSMANSHIP
DELEO CLAY TILE
DELEO CLAY TILE
DELEO CLAY TILE

(Opposite)
Design Firm: Mires Design
Creative Director, Art Director,
Designer: José A. Serrano
Illustrator: Tracy Sabin
Photographer: Carl Vanderschuit
Client: Deleo Clay Tile Company

(This page)
Design Firm: Mires Design
Creative Director, Art Director,
Designer: José A. Serrano
Photographer: Chris Wimpey
Writer: Kelly Smotherman
Client: Deleo Clay Tile Company

(This spread)
Design Firm: Sandstrom Design
Art Director/Designer: George Vogt
Illustrator: Greg Clarke
Writer: Jack Harding
Client: California Marriott Hotels, Katsin/Loeb Advertising
Description: Targeting top meeting planners, this wooden clock has a face that is a removable work of art by a California illustrator; each month the planner received a new face, along with seasonal offers. On the back of the clock, five cards rotate into view with details on each resort.

twelve
1
11
2
10
9
3
8
4
7
6
5

(This page)
Design Firm: Hornall Anderson Design Works
Art Director: John Hornall
Designers: John Hornall, Lisa Cerveny, Suzanne Haddon
Client: GE Capital Assurance

(Opposite)
Design Firm: Jager Di Paola Kemp Design
Creative Director: Michael Jager
Art Director: Jim Anfuso
Designer: Herb George
Client: The Blue Pilgrim
Description: Skater manifesto for skateboard company

the blue pilgrim
the blue pilgrim

LIVE

(Opposite)
Design Firm: Metropolis Corporation (in-house)
Client: Metropolis Corporation

(This page)
Design Firm: Valentine Radford
Creative Director: Les Kerr
Art Directors, Designers:
Dan Birlew, Les Kerr
Photographer: Kip Lott
Writer: Jim Starr
Client: INET
Description: Invitation to INET's Supercomm 1995 trade booth

(This spread)
Design Firm, Client: Meta-4, Inc.
Printer: Anderson Lithograph
Description: Box containing a bird caller from The Nature Company

We said
we'd give you a call.
One day soon,
we'll phone.
Meta-4
THE NATURE COMPANY

meteoric
Sonicon Rocket
vaughn wedeen creative

CATCHY
vaughn wedeen creative

BRIGHT
vaughn wedeen creative

snappy
vaughn wedeen creative

(Opposite)
Design Firm: Victore Design Works
Creative Director, Designer:
James Victore
Client: Portfolio Center

(This spread)
Design Firm, Client: Jennifer Sterling Design
Creative Director, Art Director, Designer: Jennifer Sterling

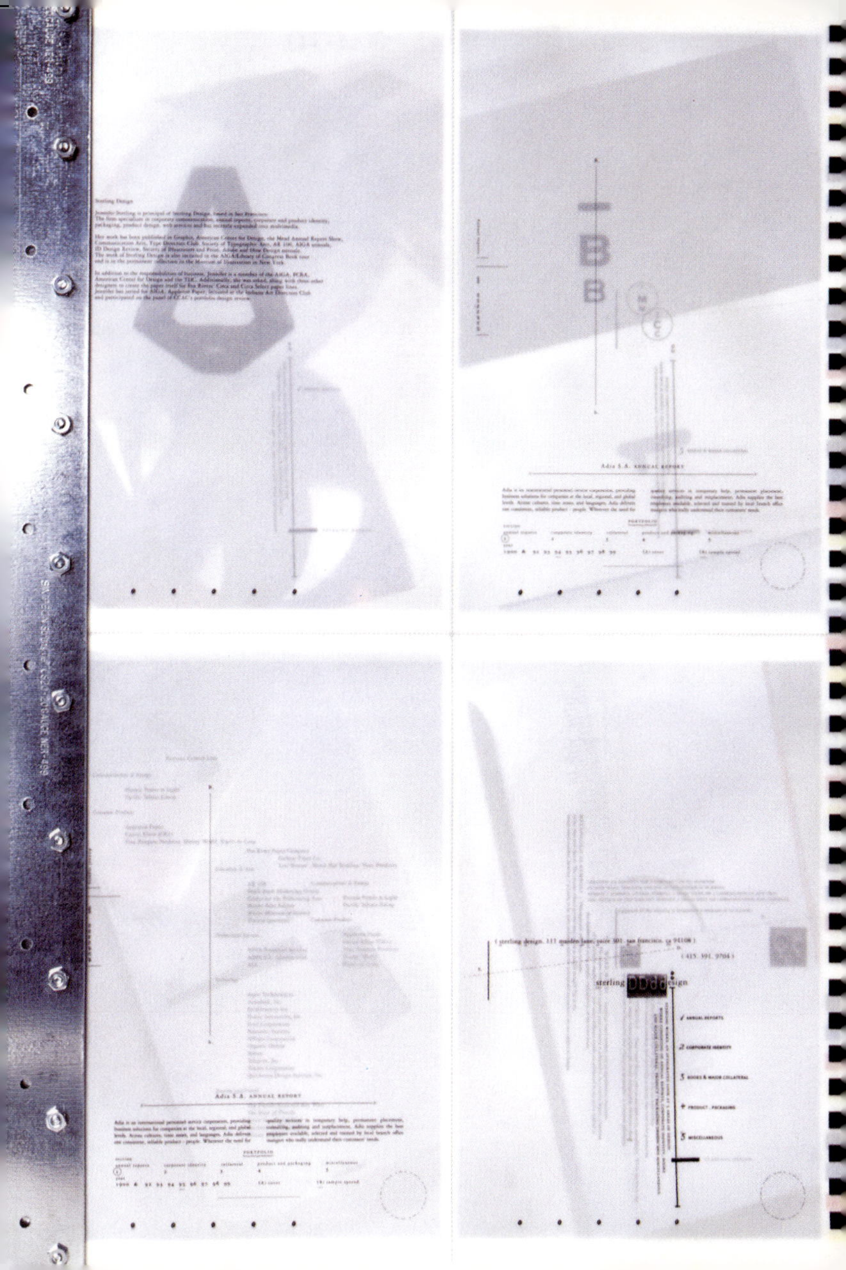
Adia S.A. ANNUAL REPORT
PORTFOLIO
Adia S.A. ANNUAL REPORT
PORTFOLIO

(This page)
Design Firm: Jennifer Sterling
Creative Director, Art Director,
Designer: Jennifer Sterling
Illustrator: Jonathan Rosen
Writer: Robert Pollie
Client: Quickturn Design Systems, Inc.

(Opposite)
Design Firm, Client: Mires Design
Creative Director, Art Director:
José A. Serrano
Designers: Miguel Perez,
Mary Pritchard
Illustrator: Christopher Wormell
Writer: John Kuraoka
Description: T-shirt for company picnic

MIRES DESIGN INC
WWW.MIRESDESIGN.COM
ENDLESS SUMMER

CASE STUDY
MIRES DESIGN INC
EAR T EAR
CASE STUDY
MIRES DESIGN INC
MAGIC CARPET BOOKS
CASE STUDY
MIRES DESIGN INC
INDUSTRY PICTURES
PICTURES

(Opposite)
Design Firm, Client: Mires Design
Creative Director, Art Director:
José A. Serrano
Designer: Jeff Samaripa

(This page)
Design Firm, Client: Vision & Factory
Art Director: Hugo Puttaert
Designers: Johan Jacobs, Hugo Puttaert

(this spread)
Design Firm, Client:
The Attik Design, Inc.

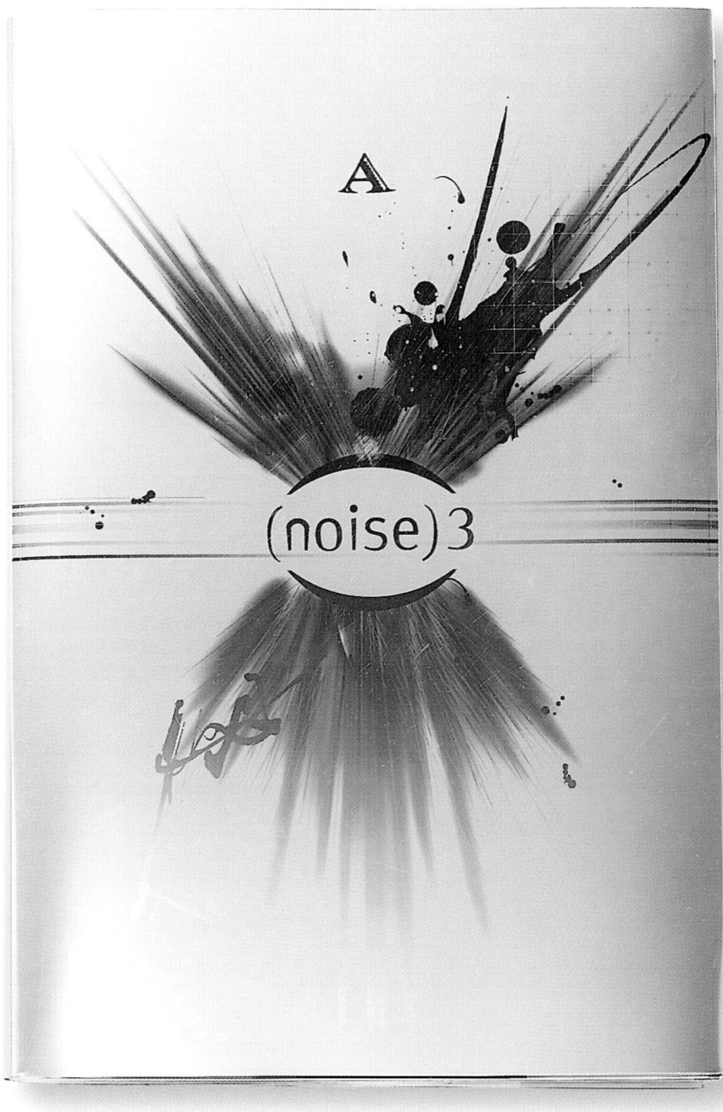
A
(noise)3

(This page)
Design Firm: Art Force Studio
Creative Director: Attila Simon
Art Director, Designer, Illustrator:
Tamás Veress

(Opposite)
Design Firm, Client: Sagmeister, Inc.
Creative Director: Stefan Sagmeister
Designers: Stefan Sagmeister, Eric Zim
Photographer: Tom Schierlitz

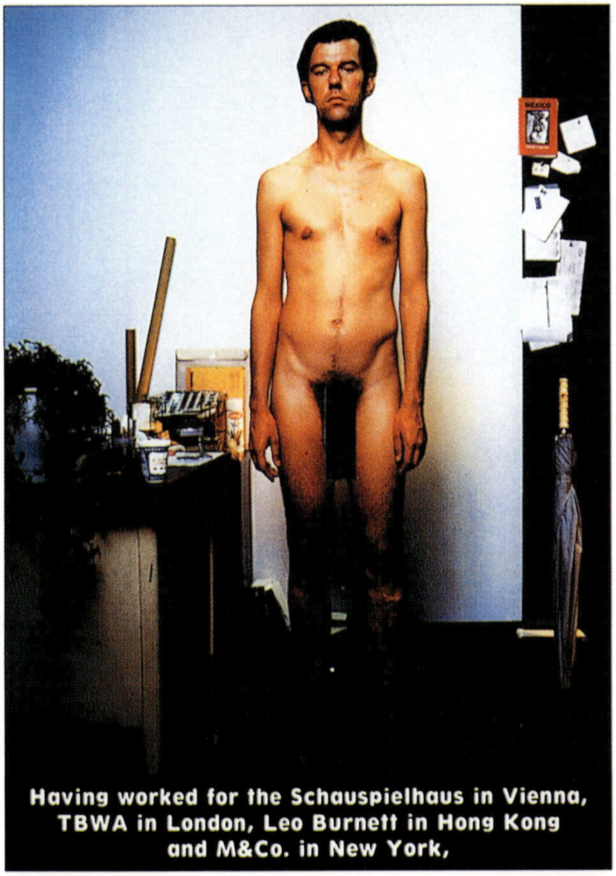
Having worked for the Schauspielhaus in Vienna,
TBWA in London, Leo Burnett in Hong Kong
and M&Co. in New York,

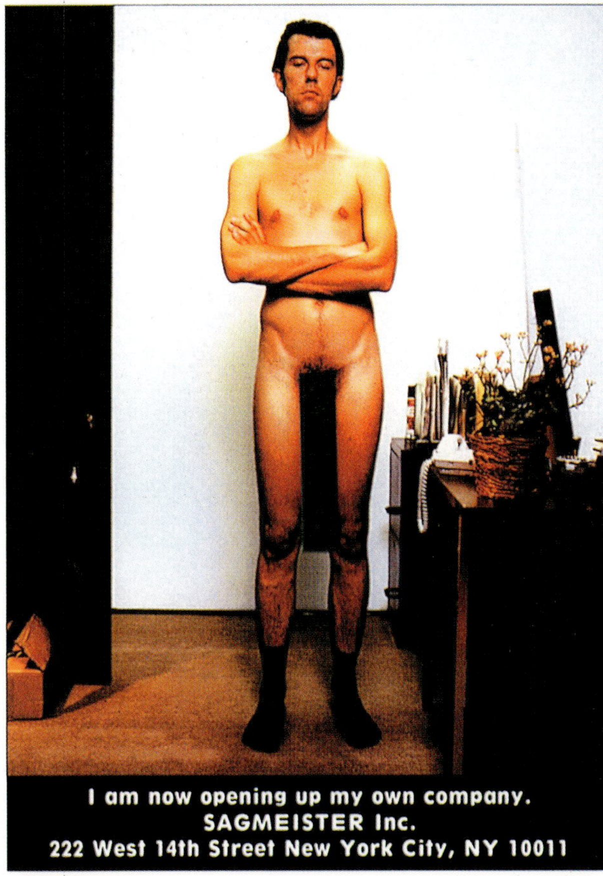
I am now opening up my own company.
SAGMEISTER Inc.
222 West 14th Street New York City, NY 10011

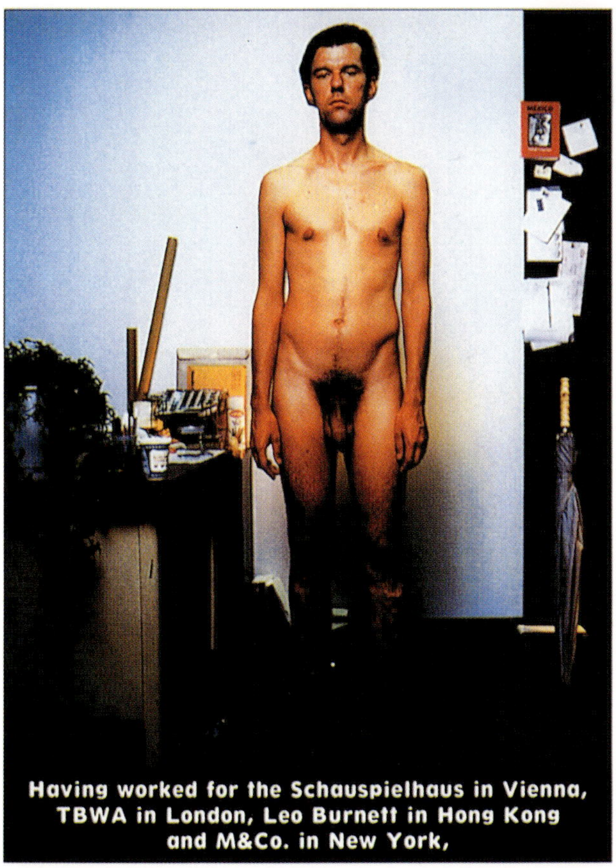
Having worked for the Schauspielhaus in Vienna,
TBWA in London, Leo Burnett in Hong Kong
and M&Co. in New York,

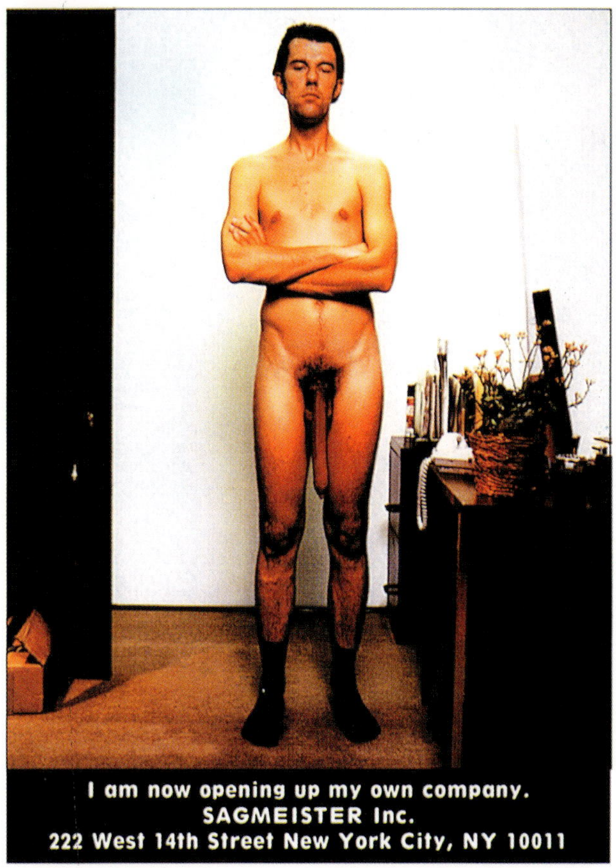
I am now opening up my own company.
SAGMEISTER Inc.
222 West 14th Street New York City, NY 10011

(This page)
Design Firm, Client: BNA Design, Ltd.
Creative Director: Grenville Main
Art Director: Jason O'Hara
Designers: Sara Williams, Diana Bidwill
Writer: Diana Bidwill
Illustrator: Watermark

(Opposite)
Design Firm, Client: BNA Design, Ltd.
Art Director, Designer: Jason O'Hara
Illustrator: Jeremy Bennett
Photographer: Alan Doak

BNA
DESIGN

(This page)
Design Firm, Client: L3
Creative Director: Lisa Ledgerwood
Designer: Travis Buckner

(Opposite)
Designer, Client: Ellen Kyung Kim
Creative Director: Kristin Sommese
Description: Résumé
in the form of a Jacob's ladder

Ellen Kyung Kim

Magazine Design, Package Design, Book Design, Time and Sequence, Computer Graphics, Applied Communications, History of Graphic Design, Design Photography, Typography, Photography, Speech Communication, Advertising, Business Writing
Applicable Skills
Macintosh:
QuarkXPress, Adobe Illustrator, Adobe
Photoshop, Aldus PageMaker
Photography:

Ellen Kyung Kim

(This page)
Design Firm: Sagmeister, Inc.
Creative Director: Stefan Sagmeister
Designers: Stefan Sagmeister,
Veronica Oh
Writer: Bob Blechman
Printer: Dave Haas
Client: The Ink Tank

(Opposite)
Design Firm, Client: The Super Market
Creative Director: Nancy Urbschat
Art Director, Writer, Designer:
David Cecchi
Photographer: David Ryan

The Super Market
welcomes this opportunity
to present our work.
We have enclosed a disc
which you will find easy
to use regardless of
your operating platform
or technical expertise.

The Super Market
Marketing Advertising Design
6 Center Square
East Longmeadow, Massachusetts 01028
tel (413) 525 0002
fax (413) 525 1258
3D
View Master

(This spread)
Designers, Clients:
Erika Schmuki, Martin Trösch

Springbrunnen und Bäder funkeln in
und Grau-Tönen, leise Musik erklin
Fenster Orangenbäume: Italien, wie e
nicht sein kann.
Mit ihrer Linken umklammert sie eine schwarze
Handtasche. Der prallgefüllte Koffer steht auf der
Waage. Erleichtert atmet sie auf: 20,8 kg. Sie
erhält ihren Pass und das Ticket zurück. Endlich
hat sie wieder genügend Zeit.
Fliegen über Dünen, überraschender Szenenwech-
sel – Felsformationen geschliffen vom sandigen
Wind. Formen so skuril wie sie sich kein Mensch
auszudenken vermag.
Klirrende Kälte spiegelt die Sonne in allen Farben
des Lichtes. Eisschichten bedecken den See. Die
kühle Eleganz des Kronleuchters verbreitet eine
Helligkeit des Luxus'.
lden ein Schie-
ahn rast darüber
hinweg. Pünktlich nach Fahrplan, dem nächsten
Bahnhof entgegen.
Rote Erde rund um den roten Dom schafft leben-
dige Natur. Eine Erholung für die Seele.
Wir sind in den Ferien vom 31. Okt bis 20. Nov
Mit freundlichen Grüssen
Erika Schmuki und Martin Trösch
Dicke Jacken schützen gegen die
riesiges Segel knattert im Wind. Eine Gischtwelle
schwappt über Deck. Wie lange die Reise noch
dauern mag?

(Opposite)
Design Firm: Vaughn Wedeen Creative
Creative Director, Art Director:
Rick Vaughn
Designers: Rick Vaughn, Pam Chang
Illustrator: Greg Tucker
Photographer: David Nufer
Writer: Foster Hurley
Computer Production:
Pamela Farrington
Printer: Color Dynamics
Client: US West

Esta es la linda tierra que busco yo,
es Borinquén la hija, la hija del mar y el sol.
This is the beautiful land I have searched for.
Borinquén is the daughter of the ocean and the sun.
From National Anthem of Puerto Rico

BIG
IDEAS

(Opposite)
Design Firm: Nike Design
Creative Director, Art Director,
Designer: Greg Hoffman
Illustrator: Ben Wong, Grey Matter
Producer: Liz Olsen
Printer: Premier Press
Client: Nike, Inc.
Description: Invitation to
Nike Exhibition on eight leading
sports and fitness concepts

(This page)
Design Firm: Anil Revri Studio
Art Director, Designer: Anil Revri
Writer: Corcoran Gallery of Art
Client: Corcoran Gallery of
Art "Friends"
Description: Invitation to fund raiser

(This page)
Design Firm: Teikna Graphic Design Inc.
Creative Director, Art Director: Claudia Neri
Designers: Claudia Neri, G. Campbell
Writer: Pamela Young
Printer: CJ Graphics
Client: Nienkämper

(Opposite)
Design Firm, Client: Sagmeister Inc.
Creative Director: Stefan Sagmeister
Designer, Writer: Jennifer Phillips

STYLE = FART. A LECTURE
BY STEFAN SAGMEISTER.
11 FEBRUARY 1998. BALTIMORE
MUSEUM OF ART. 6:15 COCK-
TAILS + LITE FARE 7PM
LECTURE. AIGA MEMBERS FREE
NON-MEMBERS $10.
GENEROUSLY SPONSORED BY
MOHAWK PAPER MILLS.
CONCEPT: STEFAN SAGMEISTER DESIGN: JENNIFER PHILLIPS

BAGS
BOTTLES
NEWSPAPERS
LAUREN
BERKOWITZ
KARYN LOVEGROVE GALLERY
18.08.1994 - 17.09.1994
Bags
go SHOPPING daily
CONSUME contents(EAT)
ACCUMULATE and SAVE over4/5
between walls 2m
alternatively, return
RECYCLING

(Opposite)
Design Firm: Fabio Ongarato Design
Designer: Fabio Ongarato
Client: Lauren Berkowitz

(This page)
Design Firm: Arias Associates
Creative Director, Art Director:
Mauricio Arias
Designer: Mauricio Arias, Karin Bryant
Client: Williams-Sonoma/Pottery Barn

You never know who's going to POP UP at this year's Halloween Party.
DATE
Saturday, October 25th
TIME
7:00pm–11:00pm
WHERE
VanderSchuit Studio
715 Turquoise Street, San Diego
(Please use alley entrance)
R.S.V.P.
Candace Daniels
at 619.539.7337
LIVE MUSIC
So bring your dancing shoes!
PRIZES
For the best costumes!
SPIRITS
and great food!
Adults only, please

(Opposite)
Design Firm: Mires Design
Creative Director, Art Director: José A. Serrano
Designers: José A. Serrano, Gale Spitzley
Illustrator: Tracy Sabin
Writer: Andrea May
Client: Vanderschuit Photography

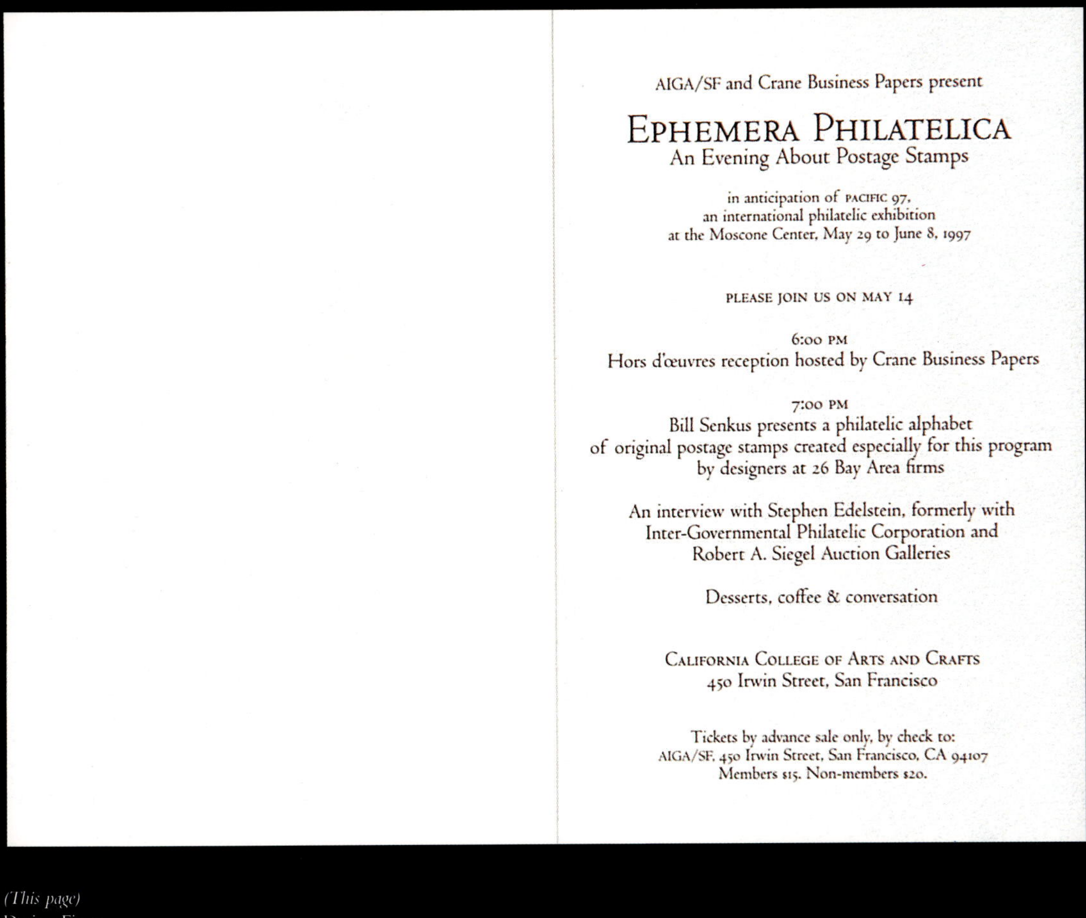

AIGA/SF and Crane Business Papers present

EPHEMERA PHILATELICA
An Evening About Postage Stamps

in anticipation of PACIFIC 97,
an international philatelic exhibition
at the Moscone Center, May 29 to June 8, 1997

PLEASE JOIN US ON MAY 14

6:00 PM
Hors d'œuvres reception hosted by Crane Business Papers

7:00 PM
Bill Senkus presents a philatelic alphabet
of original postage stamps created especially for this program
by designers at 26 Bay Area firms

An interview with Stephen Edelstein, formerly with
Inter-Governmental Philatelic Corporation and
Robert A. Siegel Auction Galleries

Desserts, coffee & conversation

CALIFORNIA COLLEGE OF ARTS AND CRAFTS
450 Irwin Street, San Francisco

Tickets by advance sale only, by check to:
AIGA/SF, 450 Irwin Street, San Francisco, CA 94107
Members $15. Non-members $20.

(This page)
Design Firm: Michael Osborne Design
Creative Director: Michael Osborne
Designers: Michael Osborne, Paul Kagiwada

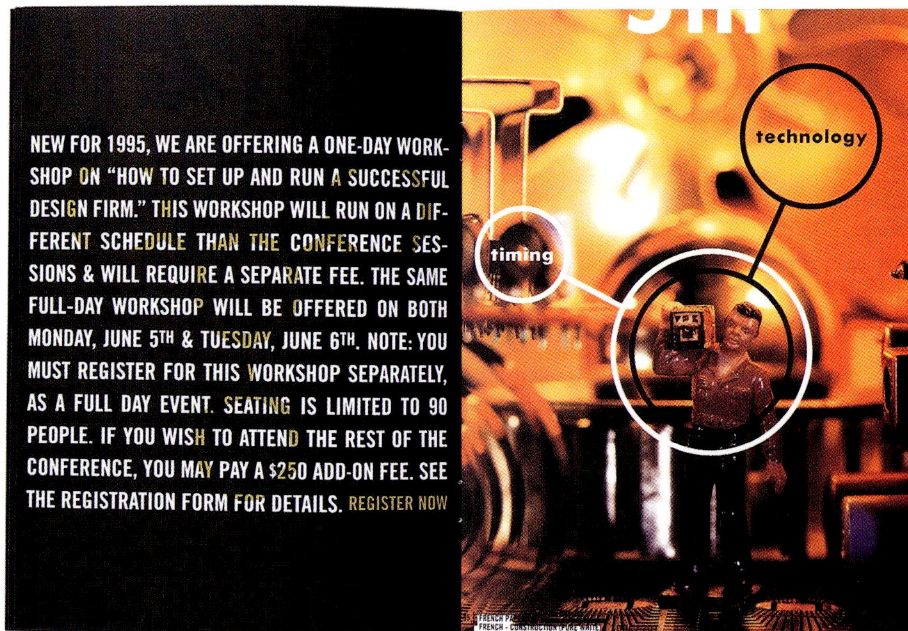

(This spread)
Design Firm:
Charles S. Anderson Design Co.
Art Directors:
Charles S. Anderson, Todd Piper-Hauswirth
Designer:
Todd Piper-Hauswirth
Photographer:
Darrell Eager
Description:
Invitation and events schedule for 1995 HOW Conference

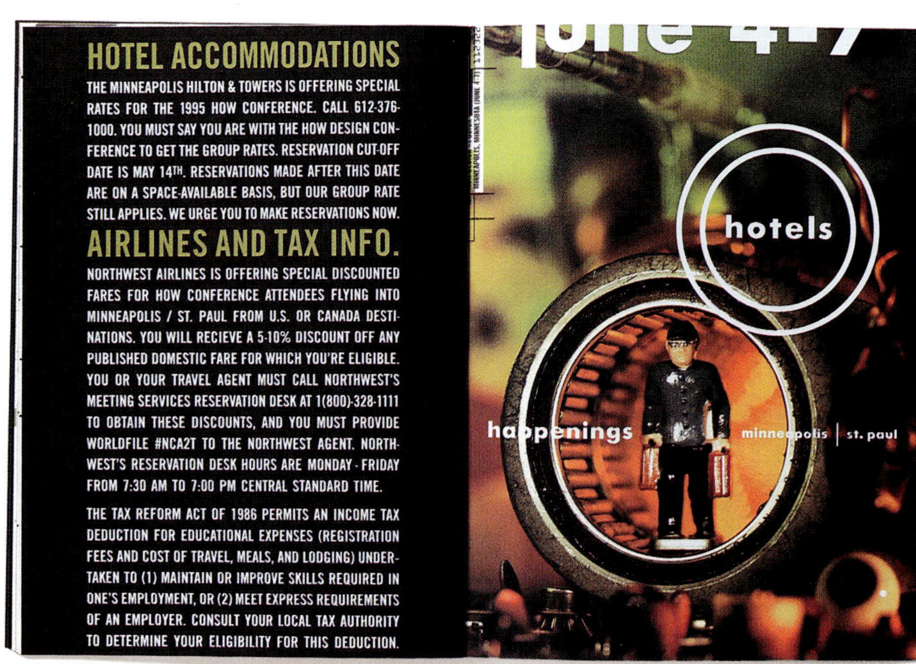

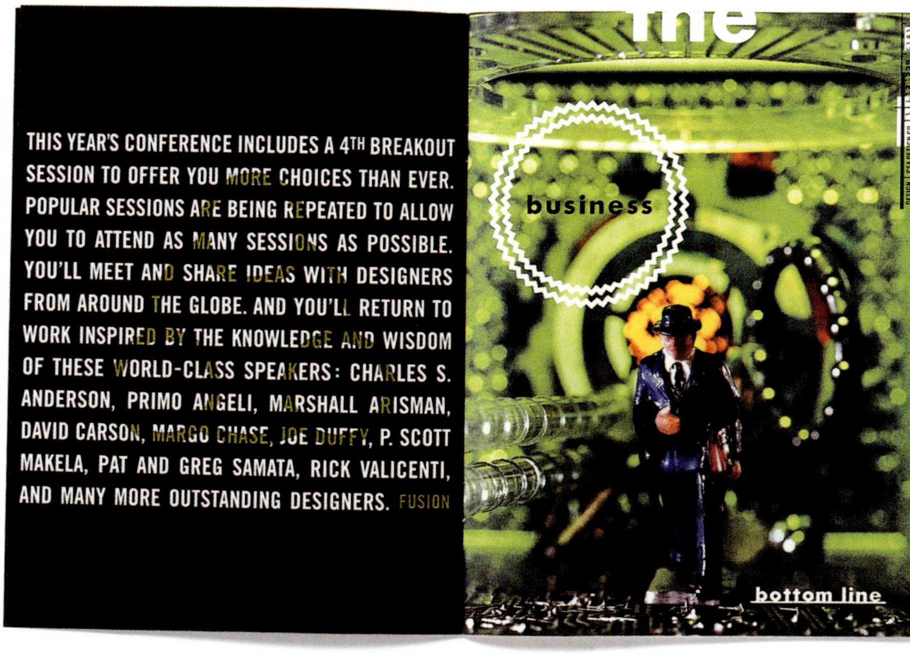
THIS YEAR'S CONFERENCE INCLUDES A 4TH BREAKOUT SESSION TO OFFER YOU MORE CHOICES THAN EVER. POPULAR SESSIONS ARE BEING REPEATED TO ALLOW YOU TO ATTEND AS MANY SESSIONS AS POSSIBLE. YOU'LL MEET AND SHARE IDEAS WITH DESIGNERS FROM AROUND THE GLOBE. AND YOU'LL RETURN TO WORK INSPIRED BY THE KNOWLEDGE AND WISDOM OF THESE WORLD-CLASS SPEAKERS: CHARLES S. ANDERSON, PRIMO ANGELI, MARSHALL ARISMAN, DAVID CARSON, MARGO CHASE, JOE DUFFY, P. SCOTT MAKELA, PAT AND GREG SAMATA, RICK VALICENTI, AND MANY MORE OUTSTANDING DESIGNERS. FUSION
business
bottom line

magazine
june
4 5
6 7

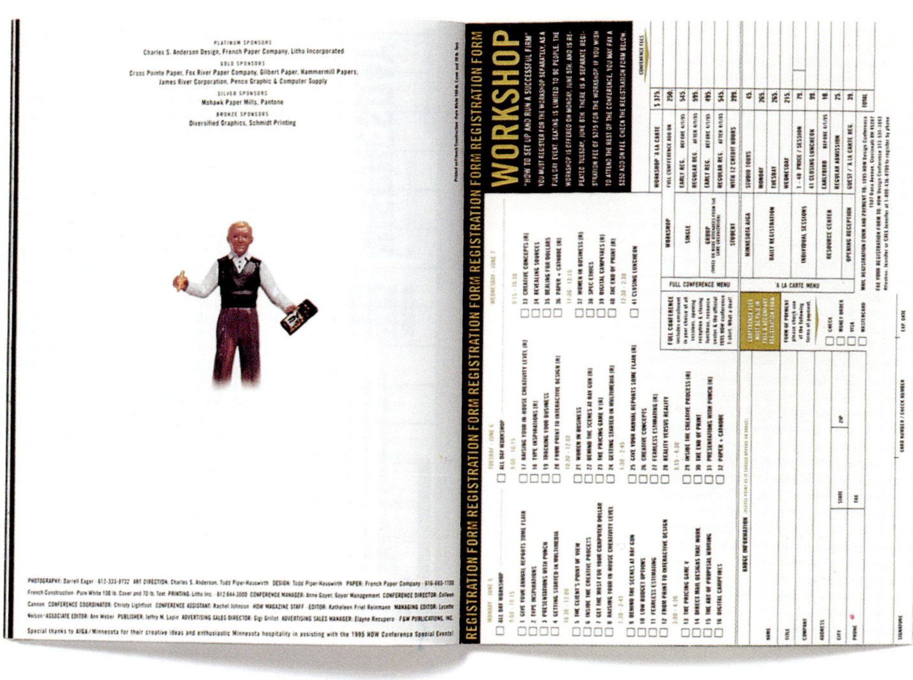
PLATINUM SPONSORS
Charles S. Anderson Design, French Paper Company, Litho Incorporated
GOLD SPONSORS
Cross Pointe Paper, Fox River Paper Company, Gilbert Paper, Hammermill Papers, James River Corporation, Penco Graphic & Computer Supply
SILVER SPONSORS
Mohawk Paper Mills, Pantone
BRONZE SPONSORS
Diversified Graphics, Schmidt Printing
WORKSHOP
REGISTRATION FORM REGISTRATION FORM REGISTRATION FORM REGISTRATION FORM REGISTRATION FORM

(This spread)
Design Firm: Pentagram Design
Art Director: Michael Bierut
Designer: Esther Bridavsky
Client: Council of Fashion
Designers of America

Special Awards
Elizabeth Tilberis "The Wonderbra" Kevyn Aucoin
Eugenia Sheppard Award for Fashion Journalism
Patrick McCarthy
Lifetime Achievement
Carrie Donovan Nonnie Moore Bernadine Morris
Special Tribute for a Lifetime of
Style and Influence on American Fashion
Jacqueline Kennedy Onassis

CFDA Foundation on behalf of the
Council of Fashion Designers of America
requests the pleasure of your company at
The 1994 CFDA Awards Gala
Monday, January 30, 1995
New York State Theater at Lincoln Center
RSVP card enclosed
black tie

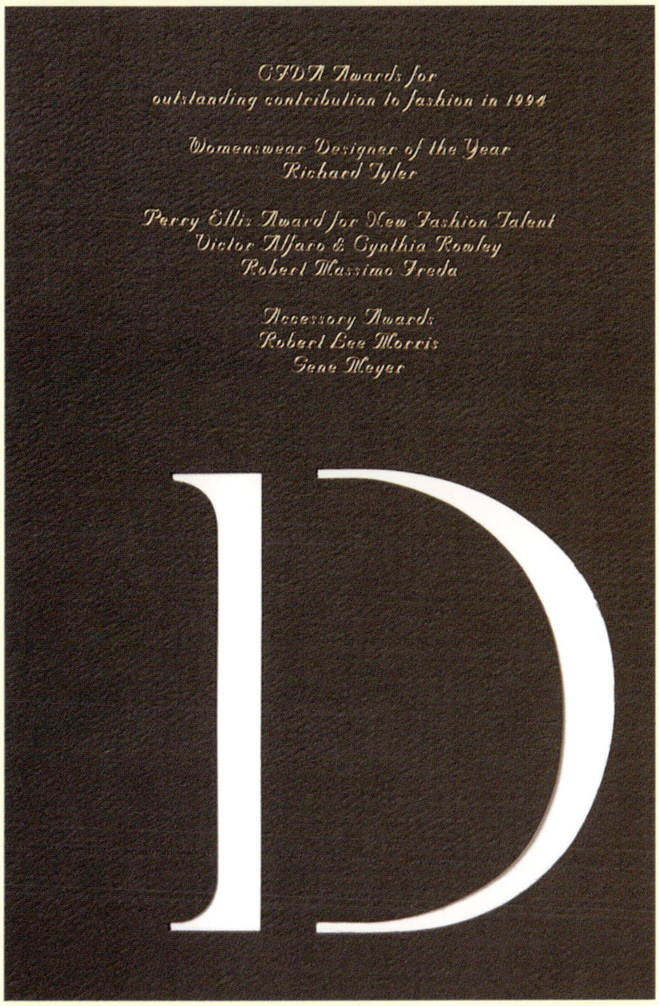
CFDA Awards for
outstanding contribution to fashion in 1994
Womenswear Designer of the Year
Richard Tyler
Perry Ellis Award for New Fashion Talent
Victor Alfaro & Cynthia Rowley
Robert Massimo Freda
Accessory Awards
Robert Lee Morris
Gene Meyer

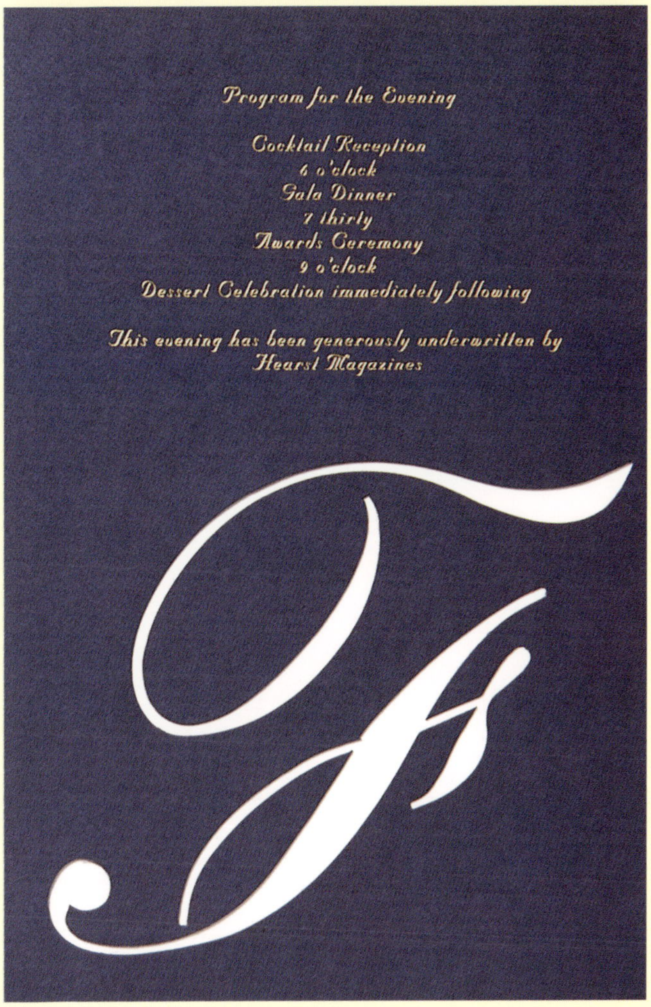
Program for the Evening
Cocktail Reception
6 o'clock
Gala Dinner
7 thirty
Awards Ceremony
9 o'clock
Dessert Celebration immediately following
This evening has been generously underwritten by
Hearst Magazines

Design Firm, Client: Squires & Company
Creative Director: Paul Black
Art Directors: Paul Black, Tom Vasquez
Designer, Illustrator, Writer: Tom Vasquez

(Top)
Design Firm, Client: Art Force Studio
Art Director, Designer: Zoltán Halasi
Illustrator: Mónika Kaszta

(Bottom)
Design Firm:
Jager Di Paola Kemp Design
Creative Director: Michael Jager
Art Director, Designer: Giovanna Jager
Client: Exquisite Corpse Artsite

DIRECT Design

DIRECT Design
ПРИГЛАШАЕМ ВАС
НА ОТКРЫТИЕ НАШЕЙ
ВЫСТАВКИ
8 ДЕКАБРЯ 1994 ГОДА
К 18.00
ПРИГЛАШЕНИЕ ДЕЙСТВИТЕЛЬНО
ВЫСТАВКА ПРОХОДИТ В ЦЕНТРАЛЬНОМ ДОМЕ ХУДОЖНИКА НА КРЫМСКОМ ВАЛУ 11 ЗАЛ
DIRECT Design

(Opposite)
Design Firm, Client: Direct Design
Art Directors, Designers: Dmitry Pioryshkov, Leon Feigin
Illustrators: Vladimir Seminihin, Dmitry Pioryshkov, Leon Feigin

(This page)
Design Firm, Client: 30sixty Design, Inc.
Creative Director: Henry Vizcarra
Art Director, Designer: Pär Larsson
Description: Party invitation

Design Firm: Art 1st Design Studio
Designer: Daniel Taracki
Photographer: Martin Szecsanov
Publisher: Vad Palmak
Printer: Keskeny & Tsa
Client: Korai Öröm
Description: CD cover and poster for Korai Öröm

Design Firm: Vaughn Wedeen Creative
Creative Director, Art Director: Rick Vaughn
Designers: Rick Vaughn, Michael O'Shaughnessy
Photographer: Michael O'Shaughnessy
Computer Production: Chip Wyly, Heather Scanlon
Client: University of New Mexico Foundation
Description: Proposal to fund art collection

An Invitation and a Gift of Glass
Barbara Lazaroff,
Glass Museum
Crest, Beverly Hills, California
1998 at 7:00pm
310.317.8600
contemporary glass art.
The Fire Transforms
directions

A BENEFIT FOR THE
Byerly's
Byerly's

(This spread)
Design Firm: Ecole Municipale des Beaux-Arts et Arts Appliqués, Metz/France
Client: L'ecole des Beaux-Arts Lorraines, France

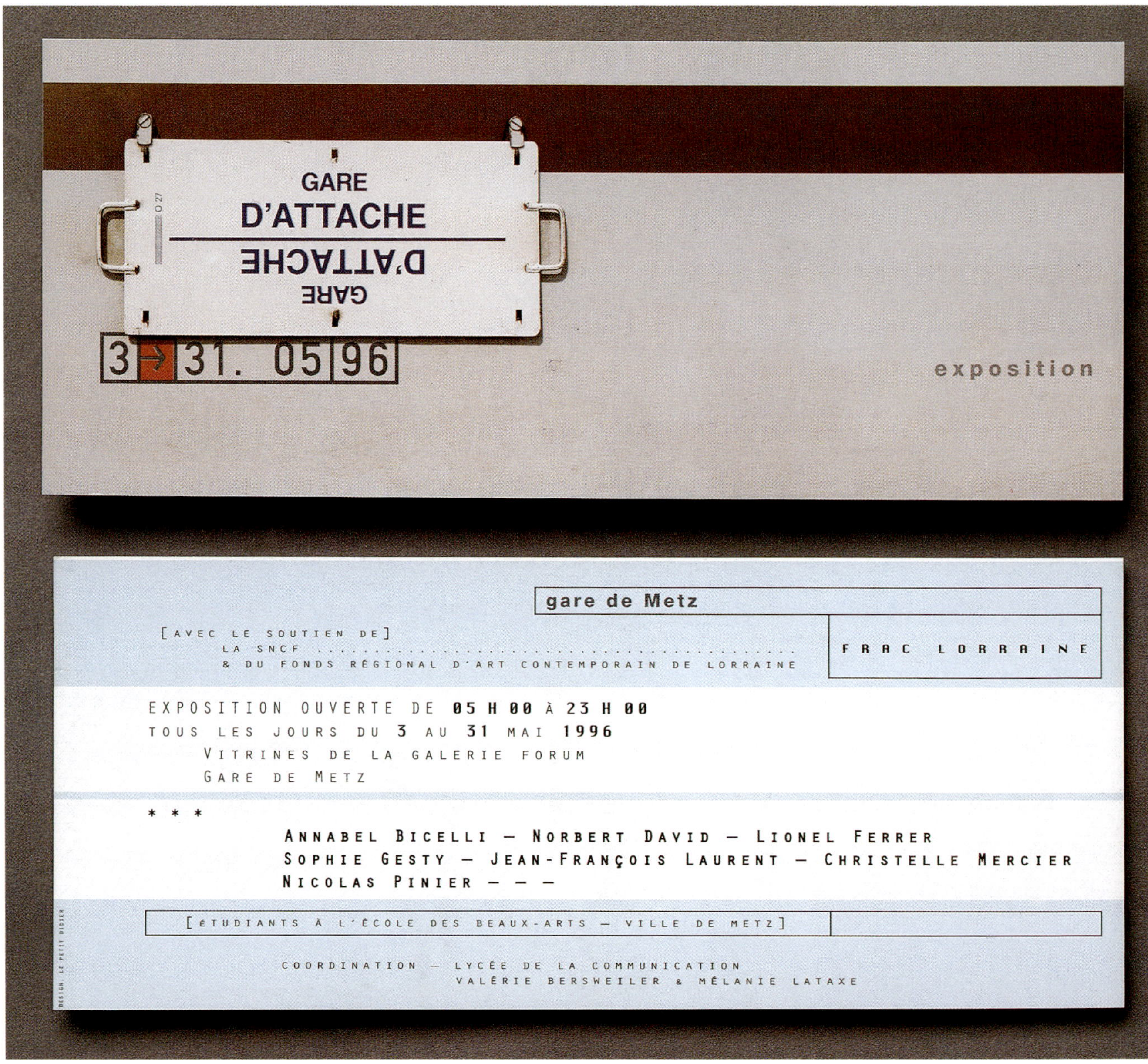

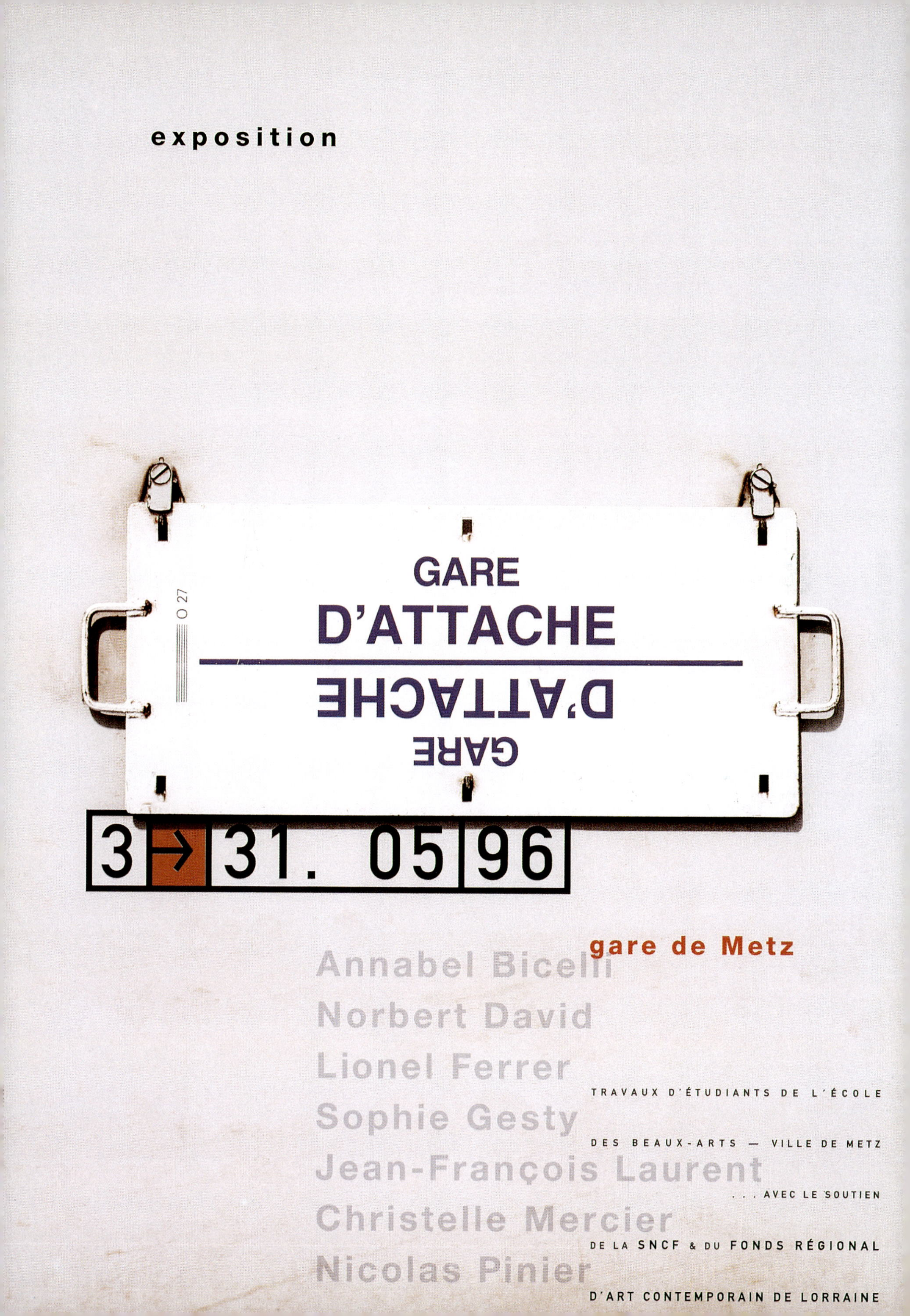
exposition
GARE
D'ATTACHE
D'ATTACHE
GARE
O 27
3 → 31. 05 96
gare de Metz
Annabel Bicelli
Norbert David
Lionel Ferrer
Sophie Gesty
Jean-François Laurent
Christelle Mercier
Nicolas Pinier
TRAVAUX D'ÉTUDIANTS DE L'ÉCOLE
DES BEAUX-ARTS — VILLE DE METZ
... AVEC LE SOUTIEN
DE LA SNCF & DU FONDS RÉGIONAL
D'ART CONTEMPORAIN DE LORRAINE

(This spread)
Design Firm: Hornall Anderson Design Works
Art Director: Jack Anderson
Designers: Jack Anderson, Cliff Chung
Client: Smith

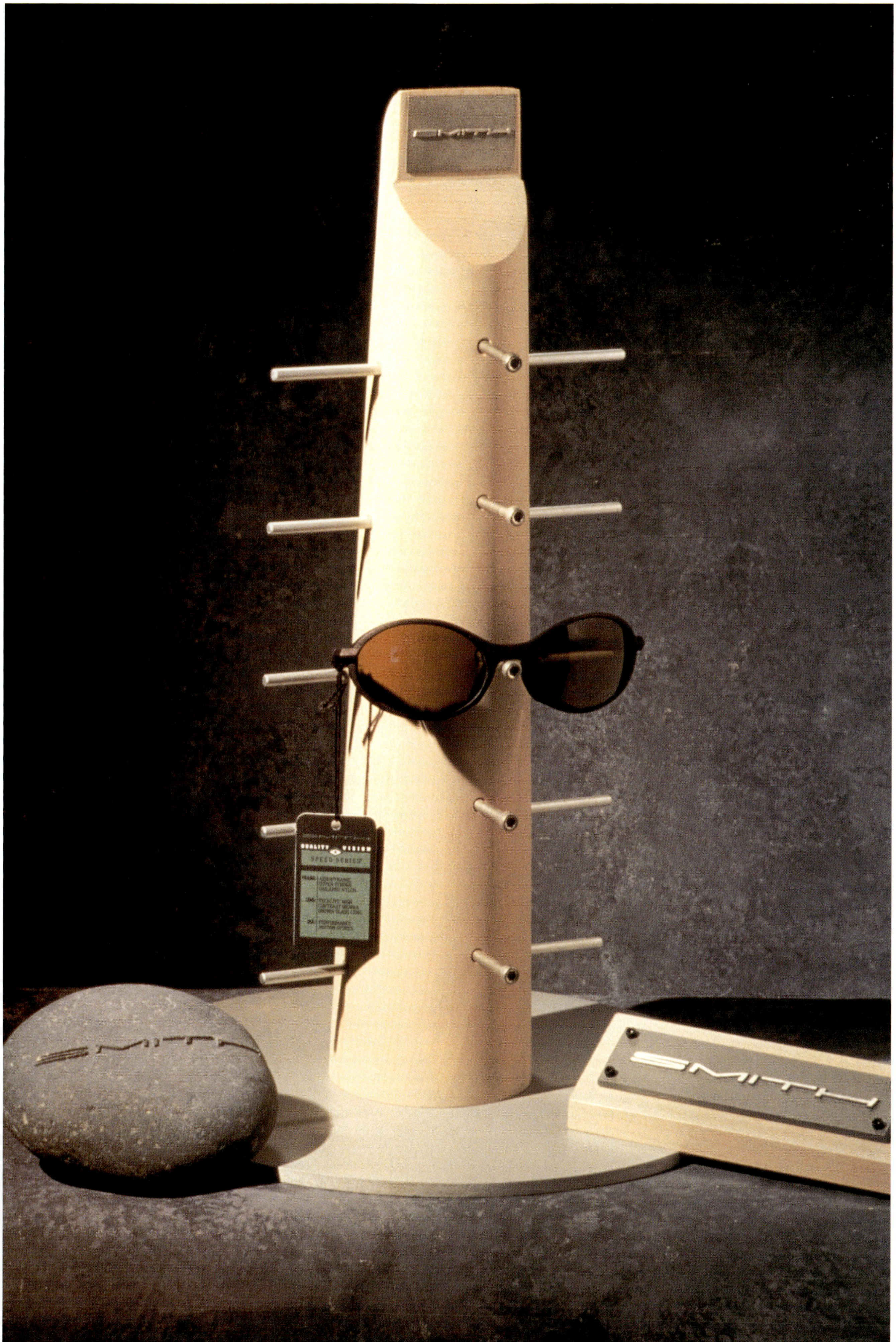
SMITH
SMITH
SMITH

basketball
basketball

(Opposite)
Design Firm: Nike (in-house)
Client: Nike, Inc.

(This page)
Design Firm: Mires Design Inc.
Creative Director, Art Director:
José A. Serrano
Designer: Jeff Samaripa
Photographer: David Deahl
Client: Big Deahl

(This spread)
Design Firm, Client: Pat Hackett,
Artist Representative
Art Director: Janet Kruse
Creative Directors: Janet Kruse,
Traci Daberko
Computer Production: Traci Daberko
Production Coordinator: Dan Snyder
Printers: Bridgetown Printing Co.,
The Copy Company

Jonathan COMBS

Dan McGOWAN

Bruce MORSER

Dennis OCHSNER

(This spread)
Design Firm, Client: Pivot Design Inc.
Creative Director: Brock Haldeman
Designers: Jim Larmon,
Brock Haldeman
Description: Flip book

designpivot
is moving
designpivot
designpivot
is moving

(This page)
Design Firm, Client: DooKim Inc.
Creative Director: Doo Kim
Illustrator: Alex Kim

(Opposite)
Design Firm, Client: Studio d Design
Art Director, Designer:
Laurie DeMartino
Photographer: Steve Belkowitz
Description: Card features Chase,
the designer's pet greyhound.

STUDIO d DESIGN IS MOVING TO MINNESOTA
DATE SEPTember 1, 1995
30 NORTH FIRST STREET FLOOR 3 MPLS MN ZIP 55401
PHONE 612 332.3987
FAX 612 332.0330
STUDIO d DESIGN
9 1 1995
MOVING TO MINNEAPOLIS
PACKAGING IDENTITY SYSTEMS LITERATURE ETC.
EST. NINETEEN HUNDRED 91
15 Spring Garden Street
Floor 1 Studio 8
delphia Pennsylvania 19123
DELIVER 2

15

Taylor Design has moved from
15 Bank Street to 51 Bank Street.

Same suite number, same city, same state, same zip,
same telephone number, same fax, and of course,
the same design standards you have come to expect.

Just remember to change the 1 and 5.

51

(This spread)
Design Firm, Client: Wild & Frey
Creative Director, Designer:
Heinz Wild

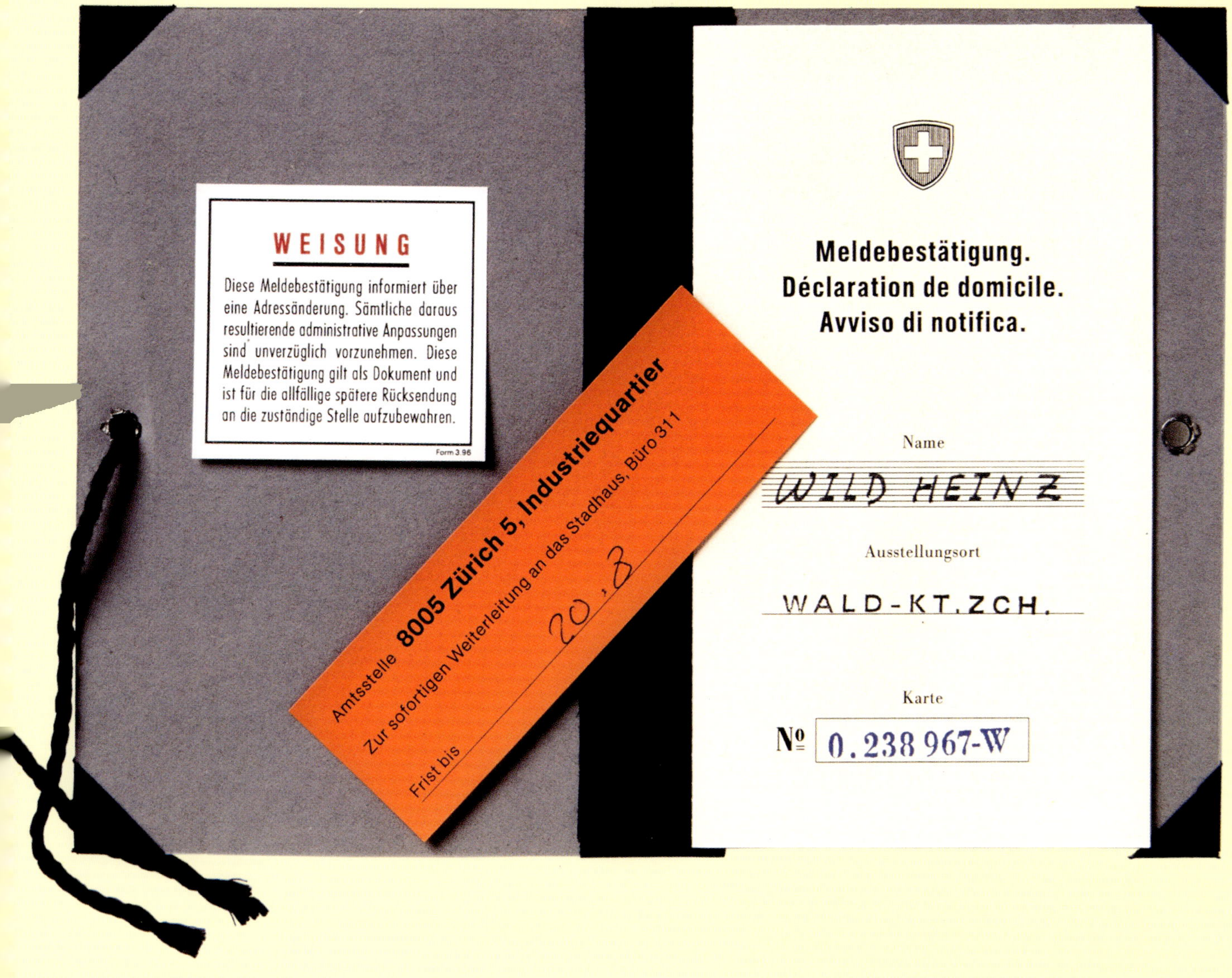
WEISUNG
Diese Meldebestätigung informiert über eine Adressänderung. Sämtliche daraus resultierende administrative Anpassungen sind unverzüglich vorzunehmen. Diese Meldebestätigung gilt als Dokument und ist für die allfällige spätere Rücksendung an die zuständige Stelle aufzubewahren.
Form 3.96
Amtsstelle 8005 Zürich 5, Industriequartier
Zur sofortigen Weiterleitung an das Stadhaus, Büro 311
Frist bis 20.3
Meldebestätigung.
Déclaration de domicile.
Avviso di notifica.
Name
WILD HEINZ
Ausstellungsort
WALD-KT.ZCH.
Karte
№ 0.238 967-W

(This page)
Design Firm, Client: A&M Records
Art Director, Designer: Karen Walker
Photographer: Frank Ockenfels
Promotional kit for radio stations

(Opposite)
Design Firm: Mires Design Inc.
Creative Director, Designer:
Scott Mires
Client: Taylor Guitars

Pick
me up!
Taylor

(This spread)
Design Firm, Client: BMG Ariola München GmbH
Art Director: Thomas Sassenbach
Designer: Martin Scharf

Herald
David Bowie
Mit seinem neuen Album OUTSIDE
kehrt David Bowie atmosphärisch zu
größten künstlerischen
zurück: den drei Alben, die er
70er Jahre mit Brian Eno
„Low", „Heroes" und
OUTSIDE ist Bowies
Projekt seit 15
Jahren, der Soundtrack zu einem
ben Charakteren seines Albums:
einem Song ist er ein 14jähriges
Mädchen, auf einem anderen
heruntergekommener, fast
Jahre alter Greis, auf einem dritten
ein 46jähriger tyrannischer Futurist.
Erst jetzt, da er selbst in die besten
Jahre kommt, kann Bowie
machen, die
Jungen eben
Nikon
LUCKY STRIKE

(This page)
Design Firm: Design: M/W
Creative Director: J. Phillips Williams
Designers: Allison Muench Williams, Peter Phong
Illustrator: Peter Phong

Client: Crane Business Papers
Description: Invitation to discussion on the new marketing role for business staionery

(Opposite)
Design Firm: Mires Design Inc.
Creative Director, Art Director: José A. Serrano
Designers: José A. Serrano, Miguel Perez
Illustrator: Tracy Sabin
Client: Green Field Paper Company

WRITE STUFF
RECYCLED KRAFT WRITING PAPER
100% POST CONSUMER
12 BUSINESS SIZE ENVELOPES (#10)
24 SHEETS OF WRITING PAPER (8.5 X 11)
MADE IN THE U.S.A.
LASER COMPATIBLE

(This page)
Design Firm: Vision & Factory
Creative Director: Hugo Puttaert
Designer: Ronny Reuman
Client: STORA Belgium

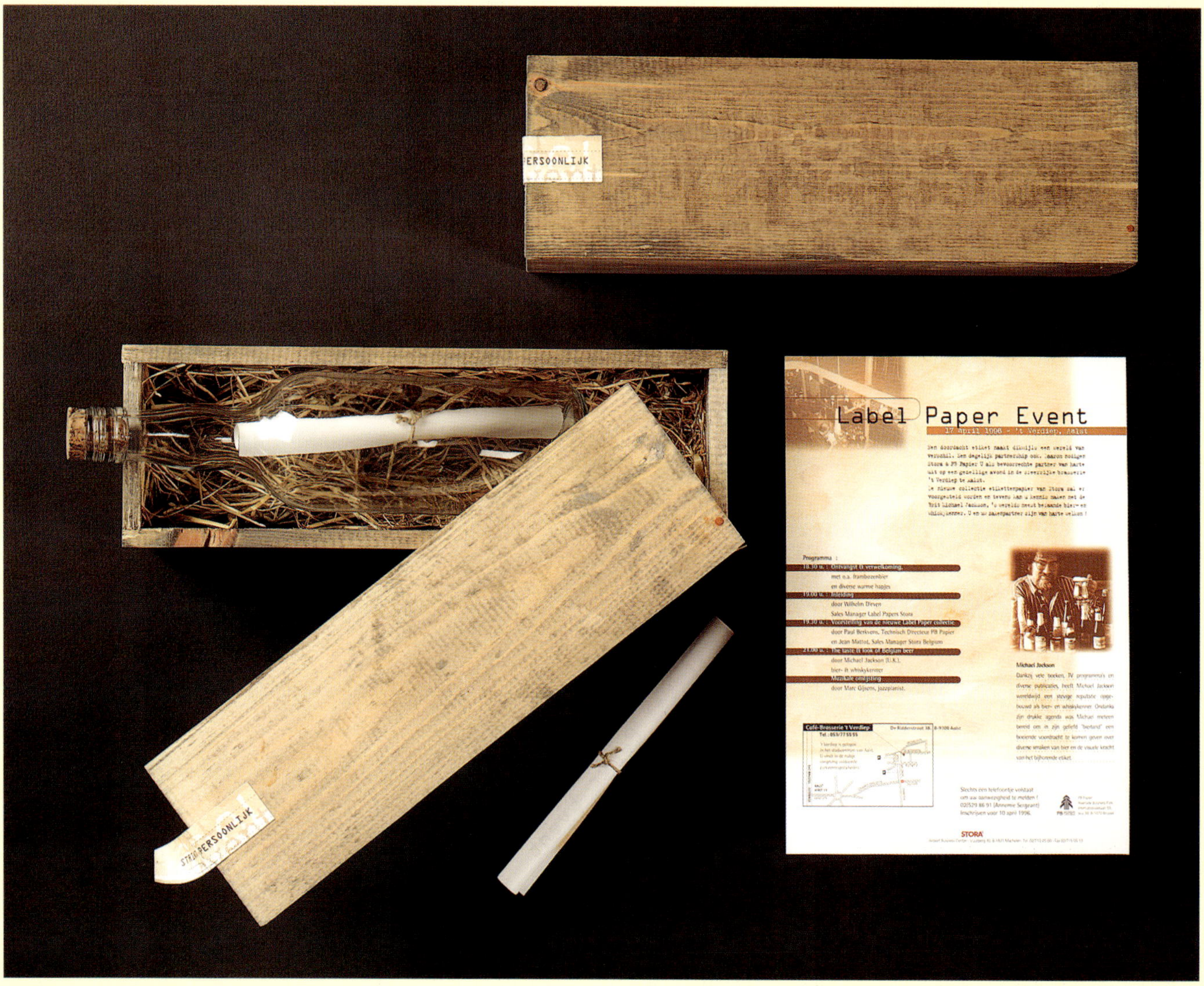

(Opposite)
Design Firm: Mires Design Inc.
Creative Director, Art Director: José A. Serrano
Designers: José A. Serrano, Deborah Hom, Mary Pritchard
Illustrators: Tracy Sabin, Fiona King
Client: Green Field Paper Company
Description: The cards have seeds embedded in the fiber and, if planted, will grow into the plant or flower pictured.

GROW A NOTE
The Notecard You Plant
GREEN FIELD
PAPER COMPANY
CARROT
SCARLET NANTES
RADISH
CHERRY BELLE
EGGPLANT
LONG PURPLE
LETTUCE
Basil Seeds
GROW A NOTE
WRITE IT · MAIL IT · PLANT IT

Bachelor Button
The brilliant, deep blue flowers of this annual heirloom are long blooming and beautiful in borders and arrangements.
RADISH
CHERRY BELLE
A brilliant red radish with crunchy white flesh which can be grown all Summer long.
Chamomile Seeds
Used medicinally for hundreds of years, the yellow chamomile flower buds produce a delightfully soothing tea.

(This page)
Design Firm: The Partners
Creative Director, Art Director,
Designer: Gillian Thomas
Client: The Association
of Photographers

(Opposite and page 240)
Design Firm: Principia Graphica
Creative Director, Art Director:
Robin Rickabaugh
Designers: Robin Rickabaugh,
Clint Gorthy
Photographer: Randy Wells
Client: Randy Wells Photography

RANDY
W E
LLS
WORLD
WIDE

(This spread)
Design Firm: Liska + Associates Inc.
Art Director: Steve Liska
Printer: Active Graphics
Client: Grubman Studios

OLD WORLD LIZARDS
REPTILES

CALL CAROLYN SONLO AT GRUBMAN PHOTOGRAPHY 312.226.2272

VOL
UME
OI

MARKO
LAVRISHA

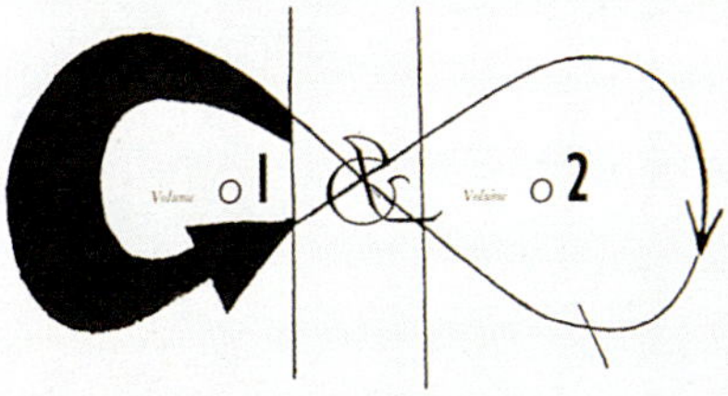

photography

MARKO LAVRISHA *photography*

MARKO Lavrisha *Portfolio of Works* is a portfolio of images. Imagine, for a moment, that they have broken free from their moorings in advertisements, brochures, catalogs and editorial to take you somewhere and tell you something they otherwise wouldn't. The best images are always trying to do that anyway.

PORTFOLIO

sections
concept 1 · miscellaneous 2 · location 3 · product 4 · fashion 5
year
1900/20__ & 98 99 00 01 02 (A) black/white (B) color

NELEMAN STUDIO 77 MERCER STREET SOHO NEW YORK CITY 10012
NELEMAN

NELEMAN

(*Opposite*)
Design Firm: The Attik Design Ltd.
Designer: Keith Seward
Photographer, Client: Hans Neleman

(*This page*)
Designer, Photographer: Joseph Szalai
Client: Benoit De Gorski
Description: Photo from promotion for a jewelry store.

Her Instincts Remembered.

Objects. In The Mind of the Beholder.

Poised For Composition.

(This spread)
Design Firm: GibbsBaronet
Creative Director: Steve Gibbs
Photographer, Client: Andy Post

VIEL GLÜCK IM NEUEN JAHR

GRITZBACH FOTOGRAF LANGE REIHE 88 2000 HAMBURG 1 249002

VIEL GLÜCK IM NEUEN JAHR

GRITZBACH FOTOGRAF LANGE REIHE 88 20099 HAMBURG 249002

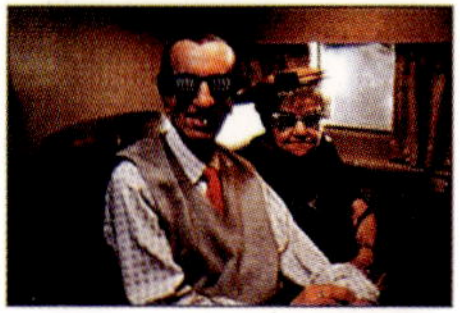

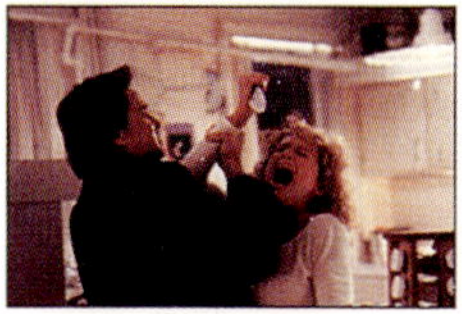

ANDY SCHWARTZ PHOTOGRAPHY
212-947-0485

AN EDITION OF 12 POSTAL CARDS
WITH PHOTOGRAPHS BY:
GEOF KERN
Number 341 in a limited edition of
1,000
All photographs ©1996 by Geof Kern.
All rights reserved under International and Pan-American Copyright Conventions.
CATALOG
[1]
Anonymous Men
From a series photographed in the South of England for the department store Neiman Marcus, for an advertising insert in Gentleman's Quarterly, Fall 1995.
Reproduced from an 8"x 10" black & white print
[2]
Coat Rack Growing Branch
From a series of photographs taken for a brochure promoting a paper mill.
Reproduced from an 16"x 20" black & white print
[3]
An Aroused Appetite
Reproduced from an 16"x 20" black & white print
[4]
Man & Woman Dancing
Reproduced from an 16"x 20" black & white print
[5/6]
Butterfly Chair; Butterfly Chair Above Trees
Photographed for Neiman Marcus as front and back covers, respectively, for the premier edition of The Book, published Spring 1996.
Both reproduced from a 4"x 5" color transparency
[7/8]
Still Life on Red; Still Life on Door
From a series of still lifes using architectural and interior elements as advertising images for a paper mill.
Both reproduced from a 4"x 5" color transparency
This assortment of 12 postal cards has been printed in a limited edition of 1,000.
This is number ________
Designed and produced by Rigsby Design, Houston; Lithographed by H. MacDonald Printing, Vancouver, BC
All photographs copyrighted Geof Kern ©1996. All rights reserved. No part of this collection may be reproduced, stored in a retrieval system, or transmitted in any form or by any means without the prior permission of Geof Kern.
Geof Kern is represented by Friend & Johnson, New York: 212-337-0055, Chicago: 312-435-0055, San Francisco: 415-927-4500, and Dallas: 214-559-0055.

(Opposite)
Design Firm: Rigsby Design
Art Director, Lana Rigsby
Designer: Michael Thede
Printer: H. MacDonald
Printing, Vancouver B.C.
Photographer, Client: Geof Kern

(This page)
Design Firm: Sandstrom Design
Creative Director, Art Director,
Designer: Steven Sandstrom
Photographer: Mark Hooper
Client: Mark Hooper Photography

Design Firm: Kuester Partners
Art Director, Designer: Bill Thorburn
Photographer: Deborah Turbeville
Client: Dayton's

Fabian Schmid
abian Schmid.

(This page)
Art Director, Designer:
Kate Cogswell
Photographer:
Charles Emmett Freeman
Client: Delphinium
(Artist Representative)

(Opposite)
Design Firm: Viva Dolan
Communications & Design
Art Director, Illustrator,
Designer: Frank Viva
Writer: Doug Dolan
Client: Arjo Wiggins Fine Papers

CONQUEROR PRESENTS
LETTERHEAD
Head and shoulders above
the competition for:
letterhead
business cards
envelopes
reports
résumés
menus
...and all your stationery needs!
CONQUEROR
FOR BUSINESSES THAT USE THEIR HEADS
POCKET
LETTERHEAD
SAMPLER
POCKET
LETTERHEAD
SAMPLER
Take One

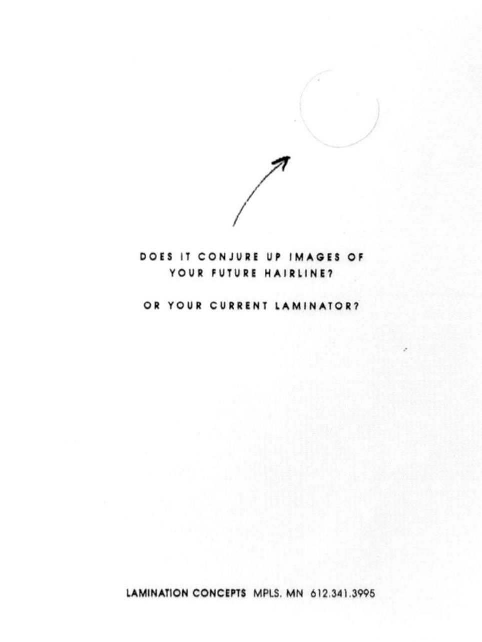

Design Firm: Clarity Coverdale Fury
Art Director, Designer: Randy Hughes
Client: Lamination Concepts

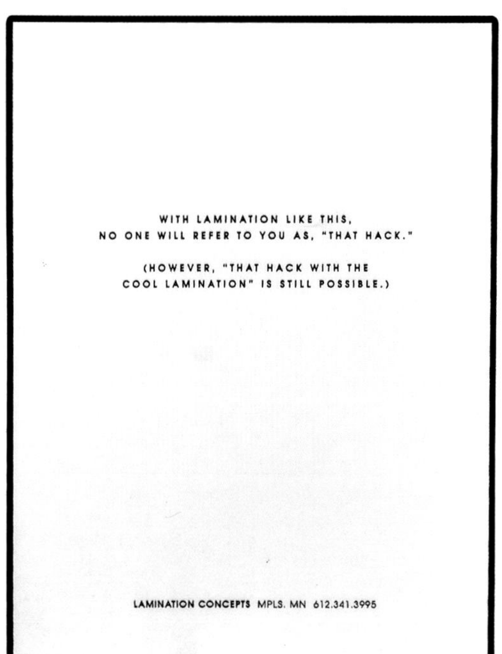

Design Firm: Peter Wilson Design
Art Directors: Peter Wilson, John Megowan
Photographer: Heinz Kohler Studios
Writer: Karen Tonnis
Toy & Comic Collection: Gary Nishimura
Client: Bremik Press

BORDEAUX
PRINTED
PRINTERS
SAMPLES

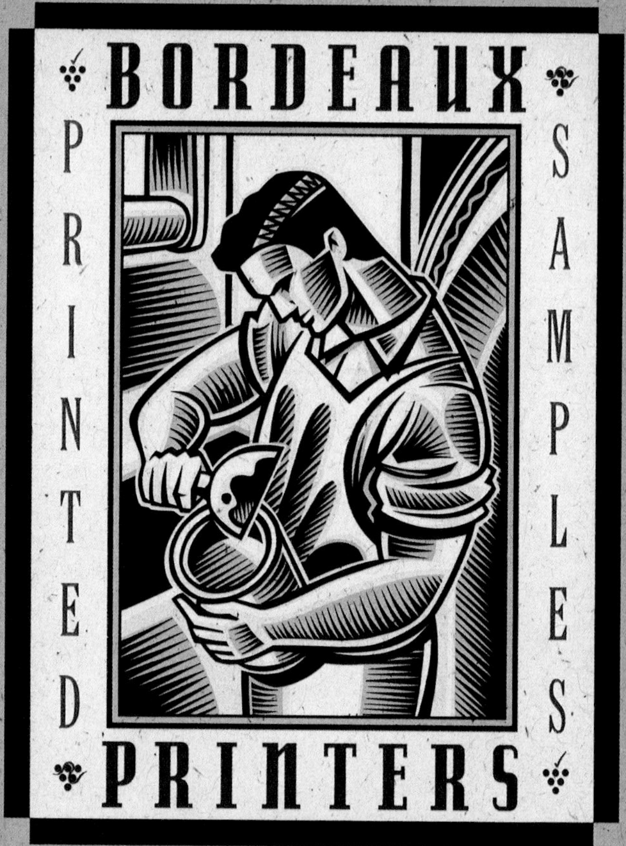
BORDEAUX
PRINTED
SAMPLES
PRINTERS

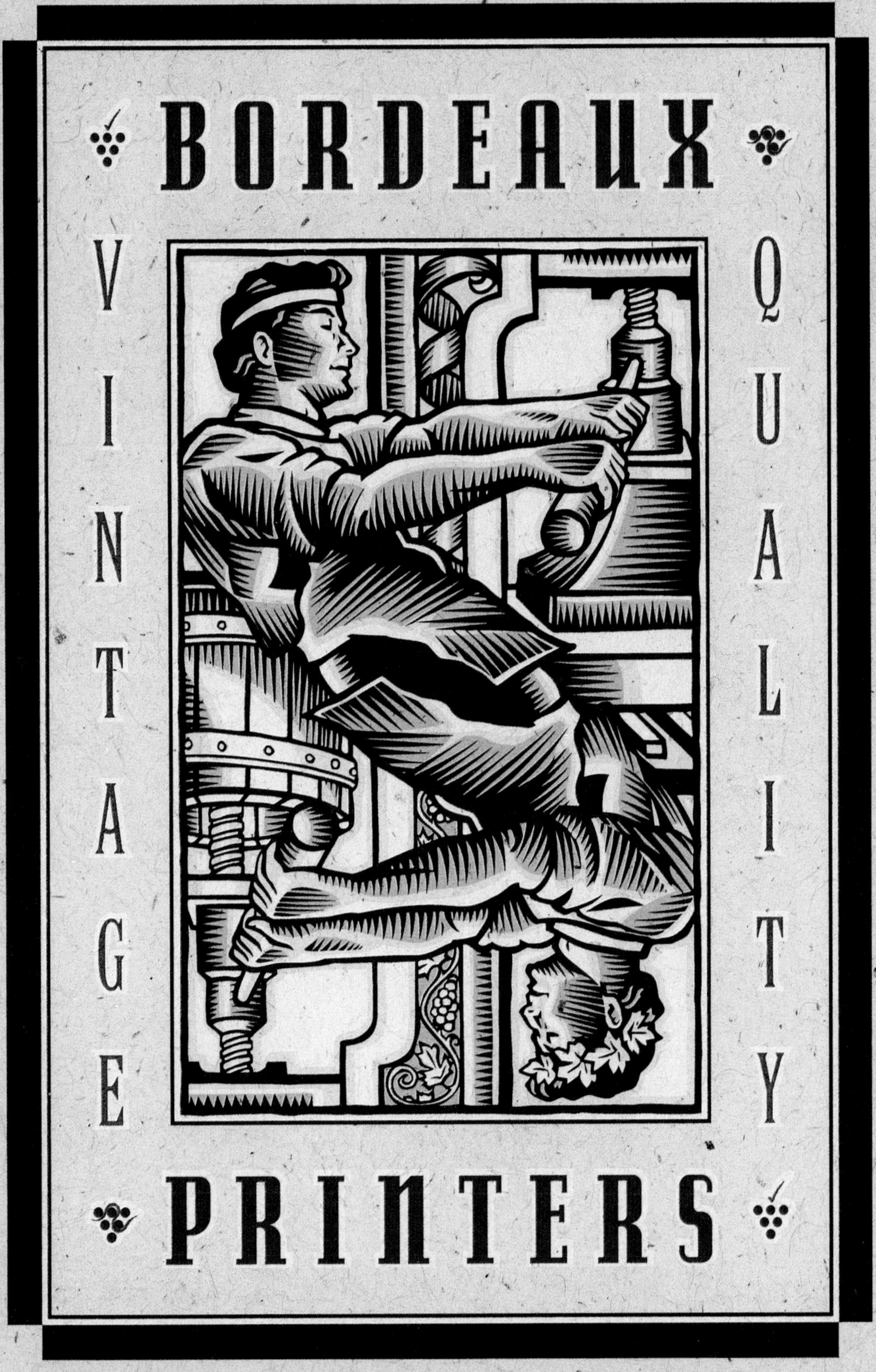
BORDEAUX
VINTAGE
QUALITY
PRINTERS

(This page)
Design Firm: Mires Design
Creative Director, Art Director:
José A. Serrano
Designers: Miguel Perez,
José A. Serrano
Illustrator: Tracy Sabin
Client: Bordeaux Printers

(Opposite)
Design Firm: Mires Design
Creative Director, Art Director:
José A. Serrano
Designer: Miguel Perez

BORDEAUX
VINTAGE
QUALITY
PRINTERS
INSPECTED BY

(This spread)
Design Firm: Susan Hochbaum Design
Creative Director, Art Director,
Designer: Susan Hochbaum
Client: Big Flower Press

BIG
FLOWER
PRESS

(This spread)
Design Firm: Pentagram Design, Ltd.
Creative Director: John McConnell
Photographers:
Amanda Clement, Nick Turner
Writer: Juliet Barclay
Client: Pentagram Papers

PENTAGRAM PAPERS 23

Before they are smoked, Havana cigars
reveal their spirit, provenance and quality through an esoteric ritual
of banding, wrapping, boxing and marking.

In 1492 in the east of Cuba two of Columbus' sailors, Rodrigo de Xerez and Luis de Torres, saw Indians smoking rolls of tobacco leaves called 'cohibas'. It was the first European encounter with the cigar.

By the end of the sixteenth century tobacco was travelling regularly from the New World to the Old. The Spanish crown enforced a strict monopoly on trade with its American territories, but Cuban tobacco arrived in England via smuggling and piracy and quickly became famous.
In the early 1600s, popular methods of smoking included 'the whiffe, the gulp, the retention and the Cuban ebolition'. Far from presenting the volcanic vision that the term implies, Cuban ebolition was the consummately elegant expulsion of a slender column of fragrant blue smoke, gently undulating, slowly rising to heaven; the emblem of the blissful contentment of the pensive cigar-smoker, lost in reflection … savouring the incomparable serenity of having found his vitola.

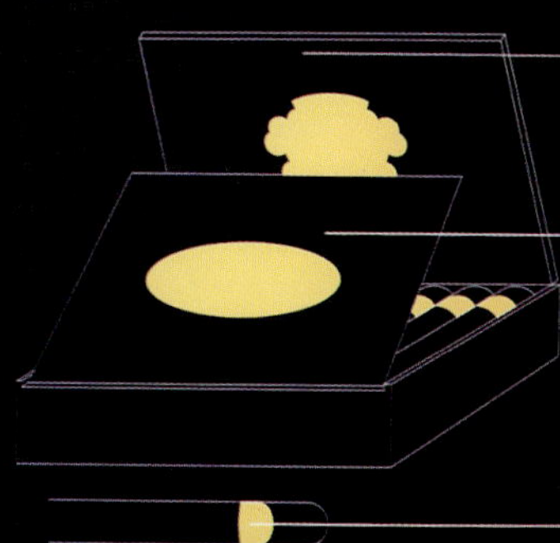

La Vista
is stuck to the inside of the lid. It is decorated with pictures and information about the brand and the factory and is often embossed.

El Bofetón
is attached to the inside of the front of the box by its lower edge; when it is turned back the cigars beneath it are revealed. It is usually only decorated with a picture, as it was designed to be seen in conjunction with the *Vista*, upon which the name and address of the factory had already been printed. The *Bofetón* is never embossed, as the texture would damage the cigars which it is designed to protect.

La Vitola
is the cigar band… but also the shape and spirit of the cigar, and the spirit of the smoker who selects it. Many cigar bands are personalised with photographs, monograms or signatures. What more perfect expression of *vitola habanera (the spirit of the habanero)* than the application of one's own *vitola* (identity) to one's own personal *vitola* (cigar band) on the cigar which has the particular *vitola* (shape, presence and identity) to which one's own *vitola* (soul) responds!

There is even *vitola* (taste, nobility and quality) in the manner in which *vitolas* are produced, with their fine drawing and rich colour.

It is no surprise that the collectors of cigar bands are called Vitolphiles.

BYRON

'Sublime tobacco! which from east to west
Cheers the tar's labours or the Turkman's rest;
Which on the Moslem's ottoman divides
His hours, and rivals opium and his brides;
Magnificent in Stamboul, but less grand,
Though not less loved, in Wapping or the Strand;
Divine in hookas, glorious in a pipe,
When tipp'd with amber, mellow, rich and ripe;
Like other charmers, wooing the caress,
More dazzlingly when daring in full dress;
Yet thy true lovers more admire by far
Thy naked beauties - Give me a cigar!

Byron, *The Island*, Canto II, Verse XIX

Researched and written by Juliet Barclay, who would like to thank Orlando Arteaga, Presidente, Asociación Cubana de Vitolfilia and Alina Gaute, Especialista, Publicitur.
Photographs by Amanda Clement and Nick Turner.

PENTAGRAM PAPERS 23

Pentagram Papers will
publish examples of curious, entertaining,
stimulating, provocative
and occasionally controversial points
of view that have come to the
attention of, or in some cases are actually
originated by, Pentagram.

(This page)
Design Firm: Mires Design Inc.
Creative Director, Art
Director: John Ball
Designers: John Ball, Deborah Hom
Writer: Andrea May
Client: Nike Inc.

(Opposite)
Design Firm: Nike (in-house)
Client: Nike Inc.

BULLS
23

(This spread)
Design Firm: Wolfback Design
Creative Director, Designer, Illustrator:
Karin Scholz
Writers: Karin Scholz,
David McDougal, John Heisse
Client: John Heisse, Karin Scholz

THE NATIONAL ENQUIRER LARGEST CIRCULATION OF ANY PAPER IN AMERICA

November 18, 1997

99c USA $1.29 Canada

Cindy Crawford downs Draino/Spam mix after devastating news of Heisse's engagement!!!

"I don't want to live" croaks desolate starlet

story, page 14

BLUSHING BRIDE GOES TO JOHN WHILE HUNDREDS WATCH!!!

Nuptials set for May '98; bride-to-be rehearses daily in Marin Headlands

It's a marriage made in Heaven.

John Heisse, globe-trotting connoisseur of beautiful women, fine wines, and long briefs, who cut a wide swath through the fields of tavern-management, lowball yachting, and the sexy-hot high-rolling world of construction litigation, finally lost his head and heart to swinging Sausalito graphic artist, brasserie-fly, and former Fightin' Owls cheerleader Karin Scholz, whose outrageous behavior on Oxford/Cambridge Boat Race Night in 1982 nearly caused the expulsion of this country's ambassador from the Court of St. James.

The couple, who plan to marry May 2nd, 1998 in Sausalito, have been cooing like a pair of turtle doves to the international press.

Heisse Presses Suit

"I ruined a great suit proposing to her," Heisse said in the tone that makes his opponents quail when big decisions about rebar hang in the balance. "She'd better marry me."

Scholz, a native of St. Louis, Missouri, and a longtime adherent of that state's "Show Me" philosophy, says "I've taken this whole relationship one day at a time. When we get to the church, we'll see what happens."

The question their friends have about the marriage is "Why are they doing it at all?" Heisse keeps a life-size

continued on page 3

Nostradamus Predicted Scholz-Heisse Union!!!

Cuneiform tablet unearthed in Cairo reveals prophesy

see page 17

ALIENS LAND in SAUSALITO: DEMAND WEDDING INVITES!!!

Martian king furious at snub!!! Scholz and Heisse stand their ground

story page 6

BRIDE CAN'T CONTAIN HER EXCITEMENT!!!

continued from page 1

poster of Madonna facing his desk in his law office, while Scholz's workstation sports a Dennis Rodman nudie screen-saver. So what gives?

Longtime friend and mad-hatter Emily Cohen whispered her theory about why Scholz is taking the plunge to this reporter in a discreet SOMA coffee-bar where the couple used to tryst.

"Well, you've seen her," Cohen murmured matter-of-factly. "Karin's only activity these days is signing up for new video-of-the-month clubs. She's metamorphosing into an epic couch-légume. It's time to get married or get upholstered."

Meanwhile Keith Bonner, who's known the groom for several decades, has a similar Heisse hypothesis. "How to put this diplomatically—? If you measured John's age in dog years, you'd have to use scientific notation. If he waits any longer, his own kids will have to call him granddad."

The Lucky Ones

The glittering guest list is nothing less than a Who's Who of international graphic design, construction law, gourmanderie, and down-market gin-mill operations.

Bob and Monnie Heisse, the groom's partying parents, are planning to tear themselves away from the spring shuffleboard season in Gettysburg, PA, to see their son tie the knot with the right woman at last. "It's about time," Monnie says. Bob concurred: "I'm tired of waiting on that boy."

Despite the fact that they've already attended one of John's weddings, the Heisse sisters, too, promise to be out in full force at the gala Sausalito event. Multimedia maven Maureen MacNeill (the glad-handing groom's little sister) and her architect husband Jeff will abandon the poultered pleasures of chicken capital Salisbury, Maryland, for this must-see/must-be-seen hymeneal hoe-down. "I'm thrilled to be going," Maureen says. "It'll give me some background material for my new TV documentary 'It's Nobody's Fault: Marital Spats in the Heart of Earthquake Country.' I'm happy for John, too. Of course."

Also jetting in from Maryland's Gold Coast will be the groom's older sister Trish Foley and her husband Mike. Trish seemed ecstatic about the coming conjugational carnival. "I've never been to Los Angeles! Maybe I'll see Tom Cruise!"

Rounding out the Heisse sisters are Kathy and Mary, who took their sibling rivalry seriously (and took lack of imagination to new depths) by marrying twin brothers Joe and Rene Laurel. When asked to comment on the prospect of yet another Heisse marriage, Kathy replied, "Well, at least John doesn't have a twin brother; at least not that we know of."

Jack Wilhelm, "Uncle Jack" the Dancing Duffer, another Marylander, is said to be "50 percent sure" he can tear himself away from his Saturday stamp collecting class to attend the ceremony, but is making no commitments. Uncle Jack Heisse, on the other hand, a blood-relative and the groom's namesake, pretty much has to be there. This muscular Christian believes he's an essential component of the ceremony. "When I marry someone, they stay married," he says with a significant look. "Well, er..."

Rounding out the Heisse family contingent are two cousins, Pat Finnegan and Jim Hilferty. Both expressed their good wishes to the happy pair, and Ms. Finnegan, a long-time health-care professional, added, "I'm planning on taking the day off for this ceremony, so if anyone needs a nurse—and knowing John, they will—have them call somebody else."

The Bridal Brood

The bride's family also intends to make the most of this party. The bride's mother, Betty Scholz, and her happy-hoofing sidekick Bruce Flood have been spotted in all the hottest St. Louis nightclubs practising their line dancing in anticipation of their big night on the dance floor. "We'll be 'Slappin Leather' with the best of them," said Betty.

The bride's proud father, Hal Scholz, and his lovely wife Mickey insist they wouldn't miss this long-awaited event. "Thank God she finally found *someone*," was Hal's comment.

Jetting in from Martha's Vineyard will be the bride's sister, Paula Conover, and, making his first ever trip west of the Poconos, her husband Gery, innkeepers to the Rich and Famous. A hotelier and antiques dealer, Conover seemed doubtful about finding anything of historic value on his mandatory trip to the West Coast. "I have dental floss older than [Scholz & Heisse's] house," he noted unhappily.

The bride's nephews, Gery Conover, Jr., who owns a thriving construction and restoration business, and Tim Conover, a prosperous investment manager, will add to the evening's quota of eligible bachelors. "Too bad all the single women will be so ancient," noted both Conovers.

Another of the Scholz sisters, Shirley Johnston, a successful drug dealer, and her biz consultant hubbie Rich, are planning a very practical gift for the newlyweds-to-be. "I'm giving John a forty-year supply of Valium and a prayer wheel," said Johnston.

Airplane mechanic and stunt skydiver Tom Scholz, the bride's wildman older brother, says he will also attend. "I'll drop in," he said casually.

Friends Weigh in

In addition to those who could not escape their genetic ties to the couple, many friends weighed their earlier vows of "weddings never again" and decided to attend the bridal bacchanalia after all.

Having survived ten days in a secluded tropical resort with the newly engaged couple last December, Emily Cohen, artist, jeweler, and sought-after social hub of the Bay Area, said she can't possibly miss this culminating event. "I'm just hoping they'll take me on their honeymoon to France," admitted Cohen.

Allison Stern, the trash-talking pocket rocket who lately raised eyebrows in the haute monde by suggesting that the Académie Française stop its foolish attempts to regulate sexual innuendo ("Who do they think they are, the Republican National Committee?"), says she'll be there, covered with jewels of her own design, and "making sure things don't get too tame. I'm not going all the way to Sausalito to do the 'Party Lite' thing, you know, chintz-and-weak-tea and people sitting around talking about cellulite. No way."

The Stanford Pod

In addition to the usual herd of empty-headed glitterati, the guest list includes a strong contingent of PhD computer scientists. Dinner Club Chairman of the Board and Squaw Valley Ski Patrol Junior Captain Hania Gajewska plans to make an appearance, though she is disappointed that night skiing won't be one of the evening's activities. "What a waste of a good mountain top," she sighed, then brightened visibly. "Of course, Karin has been known to serve good champagne from time to time."

Another of the Digerati, UC Santa Cruz professor Tracy Larrabee, whose hobbies over the years have included (chronologically) folk guitar, beading, origami, llama packing, breast feeding, and body piercing, will also deign to attend. "Karin was there for my big day," she says, "the day I first succeeded in tying a maraschino cherry stem into a knot with my tongue, so it's only right I be there for hers."

Also attending are computer-scientists-cum-musicians Amy Lansky and Steve Rubin. When the Enquirer caught up with them, they were taking time off from their Silicon Valley careers to focus on their bands full-time. Rubin's "Severe Tire Damage" ("STD" to those in the know) is notorious as the first band to play over the Internet, and, according the Discovery Channel, "the worst band to play over the Internet, or perhaps anywhere else." Lansky's band, on the other hand, is reputed to have some talent.

Another computing maven, Dinner Club member, and Severe Tire Damage member, Anna Karlin, will tear herself away from her drums, her whisk, and her polynomials to drip some charisma over the proceedings. "Yeah, I'll be there," she says with a hand on her hip and a wicked gleam in her eye. "I just hope the wedding band won't be playing Paul Revere and the Raiders," she said. "They're the group that really turn Karin's spindle."

Also among the digitally deft, search-and-rescue volunteers Linda Gass and Jamey Graham were seen in the Los Altos foothills practicing for the upcoming revels. "We'll be bringing our topological trail maps, avalanche beacons, probes, and our cadaver-sniffing dog, Zuni, in case any of the drunken

continued on page 4

A short love story

A short love story

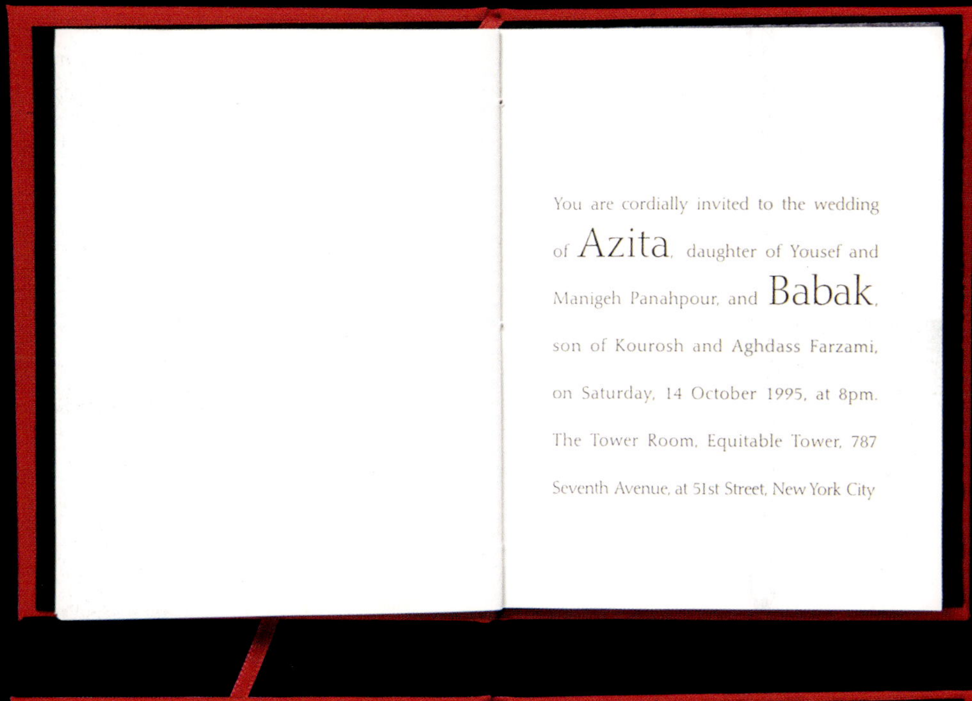
You are cordially invited to the wedding
of Azita, daughter of Yousef and
Manigeh Panahpour, and Babak,
son of Kourosh and Aghdass Farzami,
on Saturday, 14 October 1995, at 8pm.
The Tower Room, Equitable Tower, 787
Seventh Avenue, at 51st Street, New York City

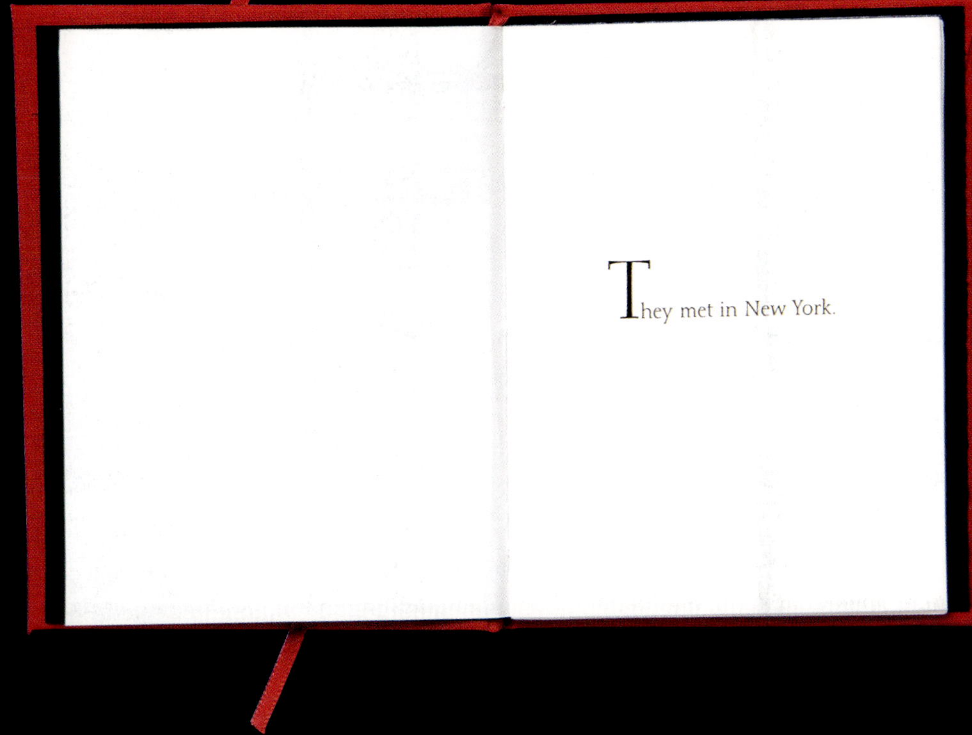
They met in New York.

(This page)
Design Firm: Boom Design
Art Director, Photographer:
Larissa Winterhalter
Designers, Clients: Larissa Winterhalter,
Joel Goldfoot

(Opposite)
Design Firm: Michael Osborne Design
Creative Director: Michael Osborne
Designer: Nicole Lembi
Clients: Alexis Woods, Daniel Donahoe

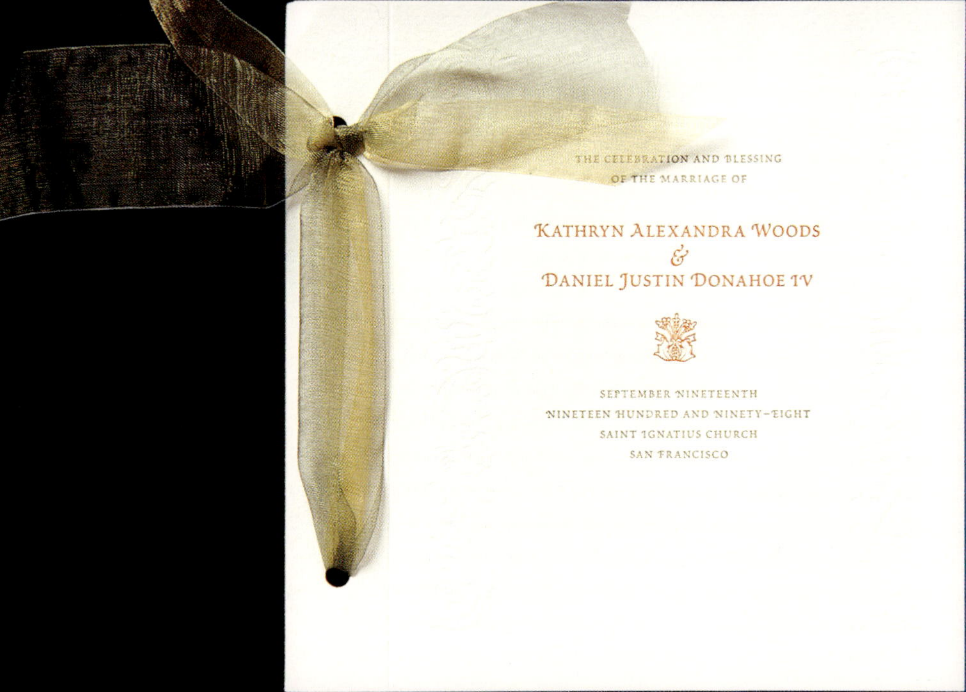
THE CELEBRATION AND BLESSING
OF THE MARRIAGE OF
KATHRYN ALEXANDRA WOODS
&
DANIEL JUSTIN DONAHOE IV
SEPTEMBER NINETEENTH
NINETEEN HUNDRED AND NINETY-EIGHT
SAINT IGNATIUS CHURCH
SAN FRANCISCO

Design Firm: Miller/Huber Relationship Marketing
Creative Director, Art Director, Designer: Paul Huber
Photographer: Gary Laufman
Writers: Sandra Watkins, Paul Huber

Client: Rich Maiers/Forte
Description: The portraits on the card overlap, and the four panels that make up each portrait can be unfolded separately to reveal parts of the other face underneath.

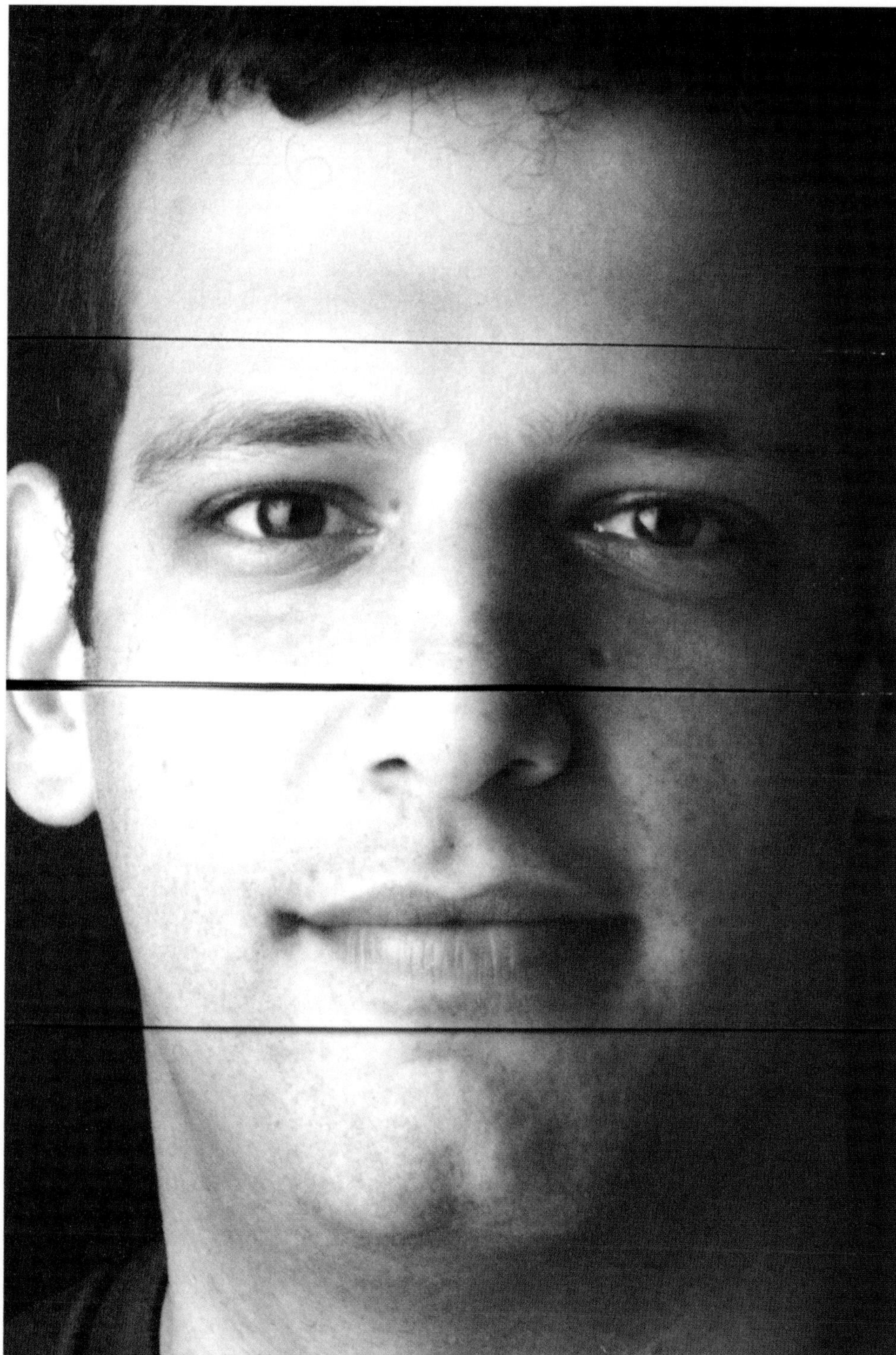

SHARON WOOD

TWO

DAVID STEINGRUBER

Celebration
two loves united make one divine
elizabeth barrett browning
in the Lord neither is woman independent of man
nor is man independent of woman
Unity

(This page)
Design Firm: Studio d Design
Art Director, Designer:
Laurie DeMartino
Client: National Greyhound
Adoption Program

(Opposite)
Design Firm: Rolling Stone (in house)
Client: Rolling Stone

10 DAYS
with this
bag
TEN DAYS
DOCUMENT

668 +

668 + 4505 + 141

180 +
5415 +
625 +
415 +

(This page)
Design Firm: Mires Design Inc.
Creative Director, Art Director, Designer: José A. Serrano
Illustrator: Tracy Sabin
Client: Cranford Street
Description: Clock for new age products company

(Opposite)
Design Firm: Art Force Studio
Art Director, Designer: Zoltán Halasi
Photographer: Árpád Bakcsy, Fotop Studio
Client: Hungarian Academy of Crafts and Design

Design Firm:
Vaughn Wedeen Creative
Creative Director, Art Director,
Designer: Rick Vaughn
Illustrator: Greg Tucker
Client: US West
Description: Internal sales
promotion package

Index

Creative Directors Art Directors Designers

Photographers Illustrators

Copywriters

Design Firms Agencies

Clients

Paper Companies Printers

Graphis Books Promotion

Graphis319
Jennifer Morla
Frank Gehry
Doo Kim
Weiss Stagliano
Ron Arad
Tibor Kalman
Mary Ellen Mark
Graphis319
MORLA / GEHRY / KIM / WEISS STAGLIANO / ARAD / KALMAN / MARK

GRAPHIS
Letterhead 4
Design Annual 1999
GRAPHIS
Annual Reports 6
Brochures 3
GRAPHIS
Corporate Identity 3
GRAPHIS
Book Design
GRAPHIS
Logo Design 4
AppleDesign
AppleDesign The Work of the Apple Industrial Design Group
GRAPHIS
T-shirt Design 2
BURY YOUR BONES
In Levi's

Order Form

We're introducing a great way to reward Graphis magazine readers: If you subscribe to Graphis, you'll qualify for a 40% discount on our books. If you subscribe and place a Standing Order, you'll get a 50% discount on our books. A Standing Order means we'll reserve your selected Graphis Annual or Series title(s) at press, and ship it to you at 50% discount. With a Standing Order for Design Annual 1999, for example, you'll receive this title at half off, and each coming year, we'll send you the newest Design Annual at this low price—an ideal way for the professional to keep informed, year after year. In addition to the titles here, we carry books in all communication disciplines, so call if there's another title we can get for you. Thank you for supporting Graphis.

Book title	Order No.	Retail	40% off Discount	standing order 50% off	Quantity	Totals
Advertising Annual 1999	1500	☐ $70.00	☐ $42.00	☐ $35.00		
Annual Reports 6 (s)	1550	☐ $70.00	☐ $42.00	☐ $35.00		
Apple Design	1259	☐ $45.00	☐ $27.00	N/A		
Black & White Blues	4710	☐ $40.00	☐ $24.00	N/A		
Book Design 2 (s)	1453	☐ $70.00	☐ $42.00	☐ $35.00		
Brochures 3 (s)	1496	☐ $70.00	☐ $42.00	☐ $35.00		
Corporate Identity 3 (s)	1437	☐ $70.00	☐ $42.00	☐ $35.00		
Design Annual 1999	1488	☐ $70.00	☐ $42.00	☐ $35.00		
Digital Photo 1 (s)	1593	☐ $70.00	☐ $42.00	☐ $35.00		
Ferenc Berko	1445	☐ $60.00	☐ $36.00	N/A		
Information Architects	1380	☐ $35.00	☐ $21.00	N/A		
Interactive Design 1 (s)	1631	☐ $70.00	☐ $42.00	☐ $35.00		
Letterhead 4 (s)	1577	☐ $70.00	☐ $42.00	☐ $35.00		
Logo Design 4 (s)	1585	☐ $60.00	☐ $36.00	☐ $30.00		
New Talent Design Annual 1999	1607	☐ $60.00	☐ $36.00	☐ $30.00		
Nudes 1	212	☐ $50.00	☐ $30.00	N/A		
Passion & Line	1372	☐ $50.00	☐ $30.00	N/A		
Photo Annual 1998	1461	☐ $70.00	☐ $42.00	☐ $35.00		
Pool Light	1470	☐ $70.00	☐ $42.00	N/A		
Poster Design Annual 1999	1623	☐ $70.00	☐ $42.00	☐ $35.00		
Product Design 2 (s)	1330	☐ $70.00	☐ $42.00	☐ $35.00		
Promotion Design 1 (s)	1615	☐ $70.00	☐ $42.00	☐ $35.00		
T-Shirt Design 2 (s)	1402	☐ $60.00	☐ $36.00	☐ $30.00		
Typography 2	1267	☐ $70.00	☐ $42.00	☐ $35.00		
Walter Iooss	1569	☐ $60.00	☐ $36.00	N/A		
World Trademarks	1070	☐ $250.00	☐ $150.00	N/A		
Shipping & handling per book, US $7.00, Canada $15.00, International $20.00.						
New York State shipments add 8.25% tax.						
Standing Orders I understand I am committing to the selected annuals and/or series and will be automatically charged for each new volume in forthcoming years, at 50% off. I must call and cancel my order when I am no longer interested in purchasing the book. (To honor your standing order discount you must sign below.) Signature Date						
Graphis magazine	☐ One year subscription	USA $90	Canada $125	Int'l $125		
	☐ Two year subscription	USA $165	Canada $235	Int'l $235		
	☐ One year student*	USA $65	Canada $90	Int'l $90		
	☐ Single or Back Issues (per)	USA $24	Canada $28	Int'l $28		

*All students must mail a copy of student ID along with the order form.

(s)=series (published every 2-4 years)

Name	☐ American Express ☐ Visa ☐ Mastercard ☐ Check
Company	
Address	Card #
City State Zip	Expiration
Daytime phone	Card holder's signature

Send this order form (or copy) and make check payable to Graphis Inc. For even faster turn-around service, or if you have any questions about subscribing, call us at the following numbers: in the US (800) 209. 4234; outside the US (212) 532. 9387 ext. 242 or 241; fax (212) 696. 4242. Mailing address: Graphis, 141 Lexington Avenue, New York, New York 10016-8193. Order Graphis on the Web from anywhere in the world: <www.graphis.com>.

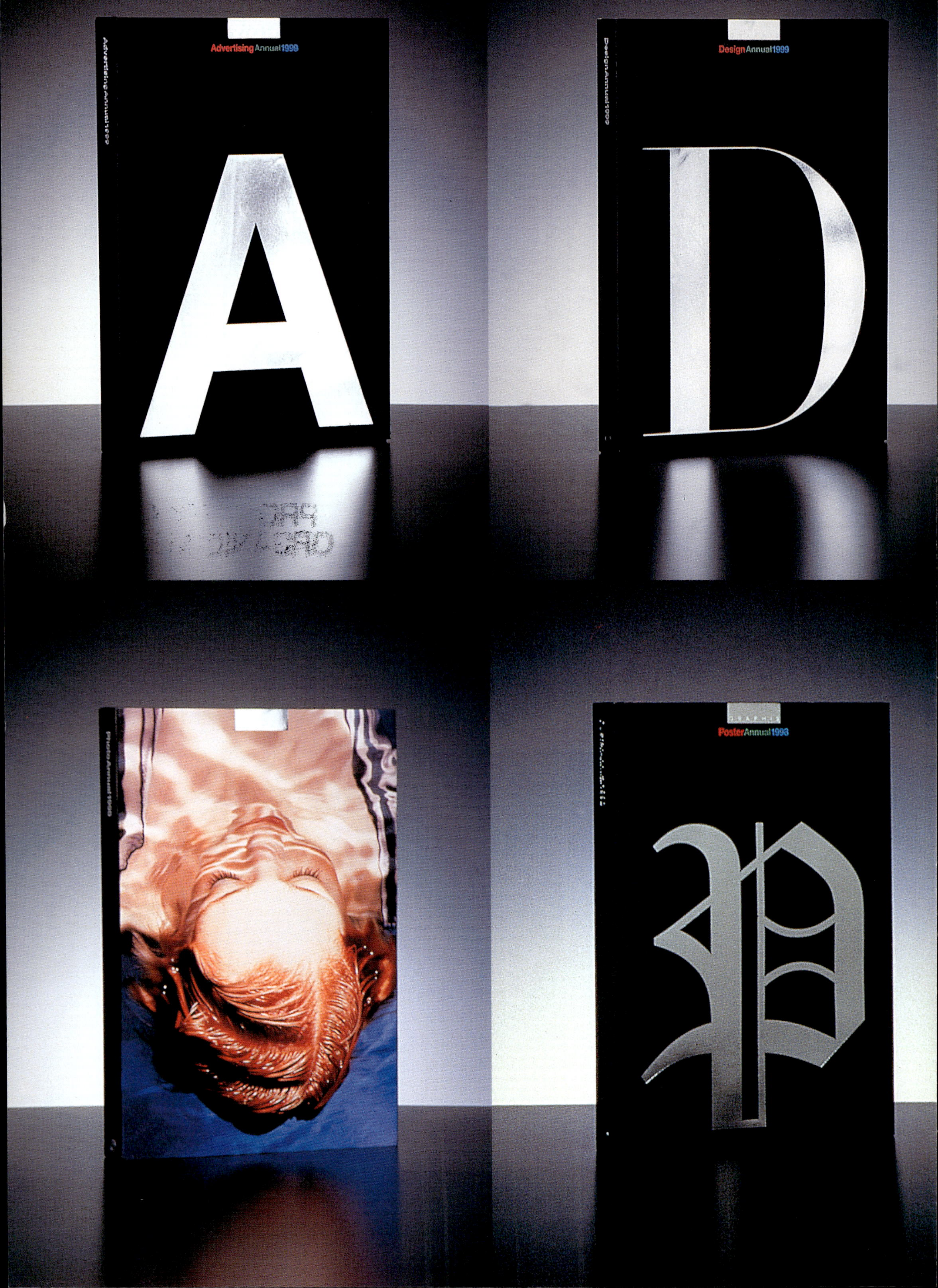
Advertising Annual1999
Design Annual1999
GRAPHIS
Poster Annual1998

Graphis Books Call For Entry

If you would like us to put you on our Call for Entries mailing list for any of our books, please fill out the form and check off the specific books of which you would like to be a part. We now consolidate our mailings twice a year for our spring and fall books. If information is needed on specific deadlines for any of our books, please consult our website: www.graphis.com.

Graphic Design Books
- ☐ Advertising Annual
- ☐ Annual Reports
- ☐ Book Design
- ☐ Brochure
- ☐ Corporate Identity
- ☐ Design Annual
- ☐ Digital Fonts
- ☐ Diagrams
- ☐ Poster Annual
- ☐ Products by Design
- ☐ Letterhead
- ☐ Logo Design
- ☐ Music CD
- ☐ New Media
- ☐ Packaging
- ☐ Paper Promotions
- ☐ Typography

Photography Books
- ☐ Digital Photo (Professional)
- ☐ Human Cond. (Photojournalism)
- ☐ New Talent (Amateur)
- ☐ Nudes (Professional)
- ☐ Nudes (Fine Art)
- ☐ Photo Annual (Professional)
- ☐ Photography (Fine Art)

Student Books
- ☐ Advertising Annual
- ☐ Design Annual
- ☐ Photo Annual (Professional)
- ☐ Products by Design
- ☐ **All the Books**
- ☐ All Design Books only
- ☐ All Photo Books only
- ☐ All Student Books only

First Name: ____________________ Last Name: ____________________

Company: ____________________

Telephone: ____________________ Fax: ____________________

Mailing Address: ____________________ City: ____________________

State, Country: ____________________ Zip: ____________________

Mail form or copy to: Graphis, Call for Entries, 141 Lexington Ave., New York, New York 10016-8139, USA, or fax to (212) 213. 3229.

RANDY
W E
L L S
WORLD
WIDE